PRINCIPLES OF THE CONFLICT OF LAWS, NATIONAL AND INTERNATIONAL

PRINCIPLES OF THE CONFLICT OF LAWS NATIONAL AND INTERNATIONAL

by

K. LIPSTEIN

1981

MARTINUS NIJHOFF PUBLISHERS

THE HAGUE / BOSTON / LONDON

Distributors:

for the United States and Canada

Kluwer Boston, Inc.
190 Old Derby Street
Hingham, MA 02043
USA

for all other countries

Kluwer Academic Publishers Group
Distribution Center
P.O. Box 322
3300 AH Dordrecht
The Netherlands

Library of Congress Catalog Card Number: 81-50367

ISBN 978-94-011-8614-8 ISBN 978-94-011-9390-0 (eBook)
DOI 10.1007/978-94-011-9390-0

Revised edition of "The General Principles of Private International Law" published in volume 135 (1972-I) of the Collected Courses, The Hague Academy of International Law.

PREFACE

The present volume reproduces with slight changes the course of lectures given at The Hague in 1972 under the title of "The General Principles of Private International Law". The substance of these lectures has remained unaltered, but a number of insertions serve to corrected some formal mistakes and misprints, added references to literature, some older, some more recent, without attempting to be exhaustive, and modified and supplemented the former exposition in two respects, where subsequent criticisms called for a review. The first concerns the place of public policy in Public International Law, the second deals with spatially-conditioned or self-limiting rules in the light of recent research.

I am grateful to the Academy of International Law and its Secretary-General for their permission to re-publish the lectures as a separate volume.

TABLE OF CONTENTS

K. Lipstein

BIOGRAPHICAL NOTE

Kurt Lipstein, born 19 March 1909 in Frankfurt am Main; studied in Grenoble, Berlin and Cambridge.

Gerichtsreferendar (1931); Ph.D. (Cantab) 1936; assistant to Professor H. C. Gutteridge 1937-1941; Secretary, Faculty Board of Law 1944-1948; University Lecturer in Law 1946; Reader in the Conflict of Laws 1962; Professor of Comparative Law 1973-76; Fellow of Clare College 1956; of the Middle Temple barrister-at-law 1950; Hon. Bencher 1966; Director of Research, International Association of Legal Science 1954-1959; Visiting Professor of Law, University of Pennsylvania 1962; Northwestern University, Chicago 1966, 1968; Professeur Associé, University of Paris I, 1977-78; Member of the Committee appointed by the Lord Chancellor and the Secretary for Scotland to advise on the conclusion of treaties prepared by the Hague Conferences on Private International Law; Member of the International Academy of Comparative Law.

PRINCIPAL PUBLICATIONS

BOOKS

One of the editors of *Dicey's Conflict of Laws,* 6-8 ed. 1948, 1958, 1967.
One of the editors of Leske-Loewenfeld, *Das Eherecht der europäischen Staaten,* 2 ed.
Editor of Volume III (Private International Law) of the *International Encyclopaedia of Comparative Law.*
The Law of the European Economic Community 1974.
Editor, Harmonization of Private International Law by the E.E.C., 1978.

ARTICLES

"The Proper Law of the Contract" (with J. Brunschvig, F. Jerie, K. Rodman), (1938) 12 *St John's Law Rev.* 242-264.
"Unjustified Enrichment in the Conflict of Laws" (with H. C. Gutteridge), (1939) 7 *Cambridge Law Journal* 80-93.
"Conflict of Laws before International Tribunals I, II" (1942) 27 *Transactions of the Grotius Society* 142-175.
—(1944) 29 *Transactions of the Grotius Society,* 51-83.
"The Doctrine of Precedent in Continental Law", (1946) 28 *Journal of the Society of Comparative Law* 34-44.
"The Calvo Clause", (1945) 22 *British Year Book of International Law* 130-145.
"Bentham, Foreign Law and Foreign Lawyers", in *Jeremy Bentham and the Law,* (1947) 202-221.
"Italian Law", *Chambers Encyclopaedia* 1947.
"Spanish Law", *Chambers Encyclopaedia* 1947.
"Jurisdiction in Bankruptcy", (1949) 12 *Modern Law Rev.* 454-476.
"Recognition of Governments and the Application of Foreign Law", (1950) 35 *Transactions of the Grotius Society* 157-188.
"Jurisdiction to Wind-up Foreign Companies", (1952) 11 *Cambridge Law Journal* 198-208.
"The Review of Legislative, Executive and Judicial Acts of an Occupying Power", (1952) 4 *Communicazioni e Studi* 115-141.
"The Fundamental Categories of English Law", *Cuadernos de derecho anglo-americano* 1953.
"Legitimacy and Legitimation in English Private International Law", *Festschrift für Rabel* I, (1954) 611-630.
"A Draft Convention on the Recovery Abroad of Claims for Maintenance", (1954) 3 *International & Comparative Law Quarterly* 125-134.
The Reception of Western Law in the Countries with a Different Social and Economic Background: Turkey, I, II.
Annales de l'Institut de droit de l'Université d'Istanboul t. 5, No. 6 (1956) 11-27, 225-238.
—t. 11, Nos. 16-17 (1961), 3-13, (1957) 9 *Social Science Bulletin* 70-95.
"The Reception of Western Law in Countries with a Different Social and Economic Background: India", *Revista del Instituto de derecho comparado,* Barcelona, 8-9 (1957) 69-81, 213-225.
—(1957) 6 *Indian Yearbook of International Law* 277-293.
"The Ambatielos Case, Last Phase", (1957) 6 *I.C.L.Q.* 643-656.
"The Hague Conventions on Private International, Public Law and Public Policy" (1959) *International and Comparative Law Quarterly* 508-522.

"The Anglo-French Treaty on the Recognition and Enforcement of Judgments in Civil and Commercial Matters", *Jurisclasseur de droit international* (1960) fasc. 593, 40 pp.
"Naturalization", *Encyclopaedia Britannica* (1960).
"Protected Interests in the Law of Torts", (1963) *Cambridge Law Journal* 85-103.
"Adoption in Private International Law", (1963) 12 *I.C.L.Q.* 835-849.
(With E. Loewenfeld) "Liechtenstein gegen Guatemala, Der Nottebohm Fall", in *Gedächtnisschrift für Ludwig Marxer*, (Zurich 1963) 275-325.
"Common Law Marriage and Private International Law", *Revue critique de droit international privé*, 1964, 106-111.
"Harold Cooke Gutteridge 1876-1953", *Rabels Z.* 28 (1964) 201-207.
"English Family Law", in Leske-Loewenfeld, *Das Eherecht der europäischen Staaten*, Vol. I, Pt. 3, (1965) pp. 379-462.
"Research in Family Law", (1966) 9 *Journal of the S.P.T.L.* 217-225.
"Recognition of Foreign Divorces, Retrospects and Prospects" (1967) 2 *Ottawa L.R.* 49-70.
"Recognition of Foreign Divorces", (1967) *Cambridge Law Journal* 42-45, 182-186.
"The Tenth Session of the Hague Conference", (1966) *Cambridge Law Journal* 224-230.
"Reflexions on the Roumanian Family Code", in *Etudes juridiques en l'honneur du Prof. I. Ionescu, Revue roumaine des sciences sociales* 12 (1968) 259-264.
"Proof of Foreign Law, Scrutiny of its Constitutionality and Validity", (1967) 42 *British Year Book of International Law* 265-270.
"The Protection of Bondholders", in *Studi Ascarelli*, Vol. 3, (1969) 1159-1171.
"*Phillips* v. *Eyre*, a Re-interpretation", in *Jus Privatum Gentium, Festschrift für Max Rheinstein*, I (1969) 411-432.
"Conflict of Laws 1921-71, The Way Ahead" [1972 B] 31 *Cambridge L.J.* 67-120.
"Powers of Appointment in the Conflict of Laws", *Festschrift für Wengler* (1972).
Nullity of Marriage in English Law, *Xenion, Festschrift für Pan J. Zepos* II (1973) 401-407.
The Interpretation of Multilingual Treaties with special regard to the E.E.C. Treaties, (1974) 48 *Tulane L. R.* 907-915.
Strict Settlements according to English Law and the Swiss Land Register, a case of Transposition, *Mélanges Kubali*, Istanbul, Publ. Inst. Droit Comparé 8 no. 11, 359-369; 721-732.
Das Haager Abkommen über die internationale Abwicklung von Nachlässen, *Rabels Z.* 39 (1975) 29-55.
Conflicts of Laws in matters of Social Security under the E.E.C. Treaty, in F. G. Jacobs (ed.) *European Law and the Individual* (1976) 55-77.
Acta et Agenda (1977) 36 Cambridge Law Journal 47-61.
The Legal Structure of Association Agreements with the E.E.C. (1974-75) *British Yearbook of International Law* 201-226.
Inherent Limitations in Statutes and the Conflict of Laws (1977) 26 *International and Comparative Law Quarterly* 884-902.
The Preliminary Draft Convention on the Law applicable to Contractual and Non-Contractual Obligations, in Lipstein (ed), Harmonization of Private International Law by the E.E.C. (1978).
Un juriste anglais dans la Communauté Européenne, Rev. internat. de droit comparé 1978, 493-504.
Les Normes fixant leur propre domaine d'application: les Expériences anglaises et américaines, *Travaux du Comité de droit international privé* 1977-1979, 189-201.

PART I. THE NATURE AND FUNCTION OF PRIVATE INTERNATIONAL LAW

Section 1. Introduction

1. "Gentlemen, this subject is very important. I have earned 15000 ducats by opinions given in this matter" (Baldus); [1] "the nature of the conflict of laws is a dismal swamp, filled with quaking quagmires and inhabited by learned but eccentric professors who theorize about mysterious matters in a strange and incomprehensible jargon. The ordinary court or lawyer is quite lost when engulfed or entangled in it." [2]

Unlike Baldus, I do not promise you golden rewards, but unlike Dean Prosser I hold out the prospect of exciting journeys into areas of great practical and intellectual interest. The general and specific aspects of this subject have been explored many a time in the Hague Lectures,[3] sometimes by speakers who relied exclusively on their own law, but also by those who took into account those other legal systems which are most representative in this field. For reasons which will become clear later on, the present discussion will not be confined to one legal system only and will attempt to weave into a pattern ideas and practices as they have left their mark over the centuries.

2. Private International Law or the Conflict of Laws comprises that body of rules which determines whether local or foreign law is to be applied and, if so, which system of foreign law. Both names are imprecise and misleading. This branch of the law is neither international nor private in character [4] and any conflict is notional only.[5] According to some, mainly continental, writers it also includes the law of nationality.[6] According to Anglo-American notions it comprises the rules which delimit the jurisdiction of local courts and determine the recognition and enforcement of foreign judgments. The reason is that formerly jurisdiction and choice of law were coextensive at common law.[7] The definition raises as many questions as it answers. Firstly, why should foreign law rather than local law be applied at all? The answer is that it is, of course, possible to disregard foreign law altogether, but the result is frequently inconvenient or unjust if a factual situation which has certain legal consequences in the country where it occurred originally, is treated differently in another country merely because the *lex fori* takes a different view.[8] Again, the application of the *lex fori* to situations involving strong foreign elements may lead to what may seem an un-

necessary and often ineffective extension of domestic law to matters which are outside the ambit of the *lex fori*. Secondly, are those rules of choice of law common to all countries, or does every legal system include its own rules of Private International Law? If they are common to all countries, are they common in virtue of certain rules of Public International Law? If they are not common to all countries, what is the purpose of applying foreign law if not even a semblance of uniformity can be attained by this process? These are the basic questions which must be answered at some stage for the following reason. Modern Private International Law is only of comparatively recent growth, and gaps in the law manifest themselves frequently. Moreover, the solution of a particular question of choice of law raised by the introduction of a claim or defence according to a particular system of foreign law may have to be restricted to the particular case and may not provide guidance in another case based upon an identical set of facts, but involving a claim or defence based upon the law of another country. Nevertheless, Private International Law is capable of development on a firm basis of principle more than any other branch of law.

Domestic law is the creation of national, territorial or religious units which desire to regulate in detail the social life of the community in accordance with certain social imponderables and conditions, with moral convictions and varying policies. Tradition, certainty and development are its driving forces. Private International Law, whatever its underlying purpose, has no material content. It does not offer any immediate solution for a particular dispute but operates indirectly. It only indicates the legal system which is to provide the rules to be applied in determining the particular issue.[9] It is a technique and not a system of substantive rules. Its philosophy is international or may be national, according to the view which is taken of the function and ambit of domestic law [10] and of the existence of rules of Public International Law in this matter.[11]

Because it is a technique, Private International Law, more than any other branch of the law, has been particularly susceptible to influence from abroad. Italy in the 12th, 13th and 14th centuries, France in the 14th, 15th and 16th centuries, the Netherlands in the 17th century, the United States in the first half of the 19th and the second half of the 20th century, France, Italy, Germany and England in the second half of the 19th century, have each contributed to the common technique, and it is impossible to ignore the literature and practice of foreign countries. For the same reason, the influence of writers has been more marked in this sphere of law than in any other; [12] indeed it would be possible to identify the various stages in the development of Private International Law with the names of one or a small number of persons and to trace its growth by describing the writings of various authors. A different course will be attempted here. The nature and function of Private International Law will be established by analysing the process whereby these rules were obtained over the course of centuries.

Section 2. Rome and Beyond

3. It is neither necessary nor profitable to examine whether ancient legal systems, such as those in Greece [13] and Rome,[14] possessed rules of Private International Law of the kind known to modern society. Even if they did exist—which is a matter for debate—it is certain that these rules did not influence the modern branch of this law.

Section 3. The Period After the Division of the Roman Empire—Personality of Laws

4. Choice of law became a real problem when the Roman Empire was overrun and settled by Germanic tribes.[15] These carried their own laws and customs with them, but the introduction of Germanic, especially Langobard, law in areas which formerly were part of the Roman Empire did not supersede the native Roman law, for according to the Germanic conception every person was governed by the law of the tribe to which he belonged. Thus conquerors vanquished and strangers lived according to their own laws. However, in so far as the laws of conqueror and vanquished applied within the same State, they applied not in virtue of a choice of law introducing a foreign system of laws, but because they were each of them part of the local law which was Langobard.[16] As in India and Pakistan today, so then, these personal laws constituted the local law. Matters were different where foreigners were involved. Here the difficulties in administering the law had become increasingly burdensome, as Bishop Agobard's famous complaint illustrates; commenting on the law of the Burgundians, he said:

> "Tanta diversitas legum quanta non solum in singulis regionibus aut civitatibus, sed etiam in multis domibus habetur. Nam plerumque contingit ut simul eant aut sedeant quinque homines et nullus eorum communem legem cum altero habeat." [17]

When persons, subject to different legal systems, came into contact with each other, whether through commerce or intermarriage, a cumulation of laws was clearly impracticable and clear-cut solutions were required.[18] Convenience led to the device of a *professio juris* either in order to pinpoint [19] or to select, by one's own free will,[20] the law governing the transaction.

In the end, the appearance of the newly discovered classical Roman law as a common law of the Holy Roman Empire [21] reduced Langobard law, Frankish Imperial Capitularia and the customary Roman law to special local customs [22] and destroyed the personality of laws; [23] moreover, with the growth of circumscribed local law in the city states, the *lex fori* began to assume importance,[24] especially in respect of the substance of proprietary rights.[25] Nevertheless the application of what has become local customary law was not due originally to the emergence of a notion that laws are territorial; it was applied as the law applicable to all residents, but not to foreigners, who remained subject to their personal law or to the common law (which may be Roman or Langobard).[26] However, by the end of the 12th century, the law no longer attached to a person, and the same person could be subject to Langobard law, if in Florence, and to Roman law in Bologna.[27] "Thus the former tribal laws had become elements of a conflict of laws, just as any other local law".[28]

Section 4. Feudalism and the Revival of Roman Law [29]

5. Two factors contributed to mould the Private International Law of the Middle Ages into a shape which differed radically from the earlier sphere of personality of laws. In the Netherlands and France feudalism left its imprint. In Italy, the new schools for the study of Roman Law had to grapple with a situation where local laws in force in the different regions or cities claimed exclusive application in disregard of the circumstance that the reason for the exercise of jurisdiction may have been purely adventitious.

Section 5. Feudalism

6. It would be wrong to assume that in a feudal society the *lex fori* applied to all cases which came before the local courts. True, in a feudal society the court always applied its own laws, provided that the court had jurisdiction, but the court exercised its jurisdiction only because the case was somehow factually connected with its territory. The fact counted that the defendant was resident,[30] that the act had taken place, that the contract had been concluded, or the object was situated

there.[31] Jurisdiction and the application of law were co-extensive, but it was the convenience of applying the latter which determined the former and not the converse.

Thus, by the 12th century a system had been developed in the Germanic parts of France and the Netherlands which connected persons, things, contracts and torts with a particular legal system indirectly by determining jurisdiction with the help of certain localising or connecting factors, such as place of birth, permanent residence, place of contracting or situs of objects. Effectiveness was the moving consideration, and the choice of law was coincident with the choice of jurisdiction. Feudalism and the remains of the system of personal law helped to establish it, but in the end principles of choice of law emerged which bear a remarkable similarity to modern Private International Law. This was the contribution of Germanic legal thought in the 12th and 13th centuries. It has influenced the early development in England, before the Dutch school of the 17th century made itself felt, and today a similar technique has found favour with an influential American writer.[32]

Section 6. Italy—The Legists

7. While the northern countries were grappling with questions of choice between several legal systems, none of which could claim a preponderant place, and solved them by concentrating on jurisdiction, Italian legal science [33] had to face the problem that the new common law of the Holy Roman Empire—Roman Law—existed side by side with the indigenous laws and customs of cities and regions in Italy. An early instance of the problem is to be found in the writings of Carolus de Tocco (± 1200): [34]

> "Hic nota quod alios noluit ligare nisi subditos imperio suo et est argumentum infra C.3.1.14.
>
> Est autem hóc contra consuetudines civitatum quae etiam alios constringere volunt suis statutis. Et est argumentum si litigat Mutinensis contra Bononiensem in hac civitate quod statutum non noceat Mutinensi. Sed quidam contra hoc autem dicunt argumento illo quod Mutinensis hic forum sequitur conveniendo Bononiensem unde omnes leges illius fori recipiat."

The writer was not certain whether the court in Bologna must apply its own law, the *lex fori*, to all persons and cases before it, or whether an equitable solution was required. The great lawyers of that period Azo [35] and Accursius (1228?)[36] still tended towards the application of the *lex fori*.[37] Yet this view had not gone unchallenged, and Aldricus (1170-1200) came out in favour of the "better law". He had said:

> "Quaeritur si homines diversarum provinciarum quae diversas habent consuetudines sub uno eodemque iudice litigant, utrum earum iudex qui iudicandum suscepit sequi debeat. Respondeo eam quae potior et utilior videtur. Debit enim iudicare secundum quod melius ei visum fuerit. Secundum Aldricum." [38]

Hugolinus, who expressed a similar opinion, may have limited its purport to the situation where plaintiff and defendant, being citizens of two different towns, litigate before a court in a third city.[39] Whatever its field of application, glossators and post-glossators were agreed that the clue to the solution of the problem was to be found in C.1.1.1.pr. (380 A.D.), C. Theod. 16.2.2. which provides:

> "Cunctos populos quos clementiae nostrae regit temperamentum in tali volumus religione versari quam Divinum Petrum apostolum tradidisse Romanis religio usque ad nunc ab ipso insinuata declarat . . ."

Hugolinus interpreted this passage as follows:

> "Ex ista lege aperte colligitur argumentum quod imperator non imponit legem nisi suis subditis; nam extra territorium jus dicenti impune non paretur." [40]

An inapposite text was thus employed to solve problems which it never envisaged but the principle which it interpreted was made to express was of far reaching importance. Neither the narrow application of the *lex fori*, nor the broad choice of the "better law" had in fact inspired the practice. To a certain extent the application of the *lex fori* was conditional upon the existence of jurisdiction. This could be assumed over non-residents if it was the *locus contractus, delicti, rei sitae* or in respect of counterclaims,[41] and the *lex fori* applied. Now a doctrinal basis was provided for these and other cases. Legislative power was understood to extend to all subjects, persons and objects within a particular city or State.[42] Neither the unbridled dominance of the *lex fori*, nor the uncertain operation of good sense and a feeling of justice determined the issue in the courts. An objective test, based upon personal or local allegiance (to use a modern expression), determines the choice of law. The fact that jurisdiction exists does not necessarily support the application of the *lex fori.* A first attempt in the history of Private International Law was thus made to determine the application of local and foreign law with the help of a doctrine which claimed to be of universal validity and was based upon the ties of personal and local allegiance.

The doctrine suffered from a serious deficiency, for it failed to set out in *what circumstances* the claim to apply the *lex fori* on the ground of personal or local allegiance could be asserted. This gap was filled to a great extent during the 13th and 14th centuries. A first distinction was made by Jacobus Balduinus (± 1235), followed by Odofredus, between rules of procedure (*ad litis ordinationem*) and rules of substance (*ad litis decisionem*).[43] As regards the former, the rules of procedure of the *forum* apply always and in all suits. As regards the latter, the *lex fori* is not applicable in all circumstances and without restrictions. But Balduinus failed to show in what circumstances the local law had to withdraw [44] and his distinction was not accepted without opposition, especially on the part of Accusius.

Nevertheless, the contribution of Balduinus was of great significance. While the text of the Corpus Juris encouraged the application of law based upon a division of legislative competence, Balduinus introduced a criterion to determine which legislative competence is involved. It relies on the *difference in nature* of rules of law. They are either rules of procedure or of substance, and their application in space is to be determined by the intrinsic character of the legal rules themselves.

It will be shown below that this new test is unworkable, except in the limited circumstances which attracted the attention of Balduinus himself. In those particular instances the test is still employed in modern Private International Law, where the principle applies at the present time that, where rules of procedure are in issue, the forum must follow its own rules. It became the fundamental test in the Middle Ages when, with further refinements added to it, it became known as the doctrine of the statutists.

Section 7. The Doctrine of the Statutists [45]

8. It is proper to connect the further development of the statutists doctrine with the French schools in Orléans, Toulouse and Montpelier, where the influence of Accursius, who favoured the unrestricted application of the *lex fori*, was less marked than in Italy. Here Balduinus' tenet [46] that the application of statutes in space depends upon their intrinsic nature is believed to have been given its final form. The achieve-

ments of the French school, its claim to originality and its function in the light of its political and historic background will be examined next.

9. *The French school.* One of the earliest French writers on this subject, Jean de Révigny (1270), in adding another choice of law rule to those already known in practice,[47] connected succession, both testate and intestate, with the law of the situs. In his own words—

> "semper inspicienda est loci consuetudo in quo res sunt".[48]

This hard and fast rule was qualified by his pupil Pierre de Belleperche or Bellapertica (± 1285) when he said—

> "si consuetudo est realis".[49]

Thus a second distinction had been drawn in addition to that offered by Balduinus between *leges quae ad litis ordinationem spectant* and *leges quae ad litis decisionem spectant.* Now the rules of substantive law themselves are subdivided; they are either *statuta personalia* which follow the person or *statuta realia* which are strictly local in their operation. The *lex fori* as a *statutum personale* applies only to those subject to it; as a *statutum reale* it applies to all assets situated within its jurisdiction.[50] But it does not apply to foreigners and to objects situated abroad,[51] who are subject to the *jus commune* or to the incipient conflict rule that the *lex loci* applies to contracts.[52]

The difficulty was, however, to determine whether a statute was *personalis* or *realis*; "si consuetudo non sit contra personalem obligationem inducenda sed contra realem ..." said Lambert de Salins (± 1300).[53] The answer came from Guillaume de Cun (1315-1316):[54] *statuta realia* are those which affect directly objects, *statuta personalia* are those which affect directly persons and which affect objects only indirectly. The distinction may seem plausible at first but, as will be shown below, it is often impossible to state in any particular instance whether a statute is *realis* or *personalis.*

10. *The Historical Background of the French Doctrine.* The meaning and purpose of the new distinction, said to have been introduced in France, becomes clear if its historical and political background is examined. This was the time when the Emperor's supremacy was challenged by France and Naples. The authority of the Pope to legislate with binding effect elsewhere had been challenged some 70 years before.[55] Shortly after 1250 political thinkers in France and Naples had challenged the

principle that "everyone is subject to the Emperor without exception" by opposing to it the principle: *Rex in suo regno est imperator.*[56] According to this view, within his own territory and in respect of those subject to his allegiance, the King of France as the local sovereign can legislate with effects which override imperial legislation and the *jus commune*. The purpose of the distinction employed by the French writers is now clear. Its aim is to assert the sovereign power of France or Naples to enact exceptional legislation with regard to its own territory, but not beyond. What had been hitherto only a system of interprovincial conflict of laws, subject to the overriding common and imperial law, had become a set of inter-State rules.

Thus *statuta personalia* and *statuta realia* were not mutually exclusive, as it was held later on; they are special legislation with a built-in restriction of application comparable to a modern unilateral conflict rule. Thus understood, the distinction between real and personal statutes loses much of the importance which was attributed to it later on, but it gains in clarity and significance. Further refinements were added, such as the inclusion of formalities in *statuta personalia.*

11. *The Statutist Doctrine in Italy—14th Century.* It is commonly said that the statutist doctrine was given its final form by Bartolus (1314-1357) [57], followed by Baldus (1327-1400) [58] who took over the teachings of the French school. Drawing on the canonist and civilian writers in Italy [59] and France [60] he reaffirmed the statutist doctrine,[61] but developed at the same time what may be called the equivalent of modern conflicts rules, to govern especially contracts,[62] delicts,[63] and the form of wills, more particularly where the foreign *lex causae* is the *jus commune.* Unlike his predecessors, however, he no longer treated the qualification of statutes as real and personal as a personal or territorial limitation of the *lex fori qua lex specialis.* Instead these tests now served to determine also whether foreign special legislation in the nature of personal or real statutes are to be applied in the courts of the forum. The notion now serves a bilateral purpose [64] and conflicts between a foreign *statutum personale* and a local *statutum reale* can present themselves.[65]

At the same time restrictions upon a foreign personal statute which was otherwise applicable now became necessary. Foreign prohibitive statutes are excluded if they are a *consuetudo odiosa* [66]—a forerunner of the modern doctrine of public policy:

> "Quidquid disponitur contra naturam rel rationem naturalem illum odiosum appellabitur." [67]

Baldus introduced a new line of thought when he put forward the doctrine of acquired rights as a motive and a justification for the application of foreign law.[68]

The shift towards a bilateral notion of real and personal statuta introduced the idea—not yet express in Bartolus—that all laws are either real or personal, stand on a level of equality and are mutually exclusive. Thus their application in space outside the country where they form the domestic law must depend upon whether they bear the character of the former or of the latter. *The nature of rules of domestic law determines their application in space.*

This new approach to questions of Private International Law showed itself most clearly in the controversy which raged at the beginning of the 14th century as to what law governed a succession. One party of the French school [69] believed that all rules of succession were real; another party [70] held that no hard and fast rule could be laid down; it all depended upon the wording of the statute.[71] The problem, in one form or another, has exercised the minds of lawyers up to the present day. Upon the answer to it depends whether a succession which includes assets in several countries is governed by several laws (if all laws of succession are real) or by one legal system only (if all laws are personal). The principle that a succession may be governed by several systems of law is adopted today in England and France; Germany and Italy follow the principle of unity. Bartolus followed the middle course advocated by Guillaume de Cun: *"verba consuetudinis attendenda sunt"*.[72] In so doing he exposed unwittingly the weakness of the entire structure erected by the statutists, for he argued as follows: In the case of an intestate succession of a deceased who died domiciled in England, where the principle of primogeniture applied, and who left land in Italy, where the rules of Roman law dividing the land in equal shares between the next of kin obtained, the solution must depend upon the wording of the English rule. If English law provided:

> "bona decendentium veniant in primogenitum"

the statute was *realis,* and thus restricted to the assets in England, and the Italian assets must be divided in equal shares

> "quia jus afficit res ipsas".

If English law provided—

> "primogenitus succedat"

then the statute was *personalis* [73] and the eldest son takes, subject to the exception that such a law must be regarded as an odious statute.[74] No distinction could be more fortuitous, no result could be more arbitrary.[75] The fault does not lie with Bartolus. It lies in the doctrine which he was attempting to apply. It is impossible to obtain guidance from the nature, and still less from the wording, of a statute or rule of law as to the extent to which it must be applied in space. The doctrine is unworkable in practice.[76]

It is not surprising, therefore, that Baldus refused to follow Bartolus and came down squarely in favour of the nature of all rules of succession as *statuta realia*.[77] Others, similarly bent upon avoiding the absurd result to which Bartolus' doctrine was bound to lead, invoked for the first time the intention of the deceased.[78]

To sum up: compared with the practice in Northern France and in the Netherlands, which relied on jurisdiction to be determined by clear-cut connecting factors based on residence, place of contracting, to mention one or two, reflecting the primitive concept of personality of laws, feudal ties and practical expediency, the doctrine of the statutists is strictly legal and formalistic. It had serious defects, but it was based on principles, some of which were of lasting value.

In the first place, it was *international*.[79] It attempted to furnish an explanation why foreign law is applied. This it found in the division of legislative powers between autonomous territorial units. Thereby a link was forged between the exercise of sovereign powers by States in International Law and the application of domestic or foreign law. However, the link was more apparent than real, for while the doctrine justified the power of States to legislate with extra-territorial effect, subject only to the right of other States to enact *statuta realia* which stifled the effect of foreign law, it was unable to explain why one country must apply the extra-territorial legislation of any other country. The recognition that legislative powers are divided justifies the right to export local law; it does not establish the duty to import foreign law. An answer to this problem was only offered towards the end of the 17th century by the Dutch school of writers.[80]

In the second place, it was *universalistic*. The statutist doctrine attempted to provide principles of universal application which were to indicate when foreign law was applicable. However, these attempts to determine the application in space of laws from the nature of these laws as real or personal were impracticable, since the criteria were unreal.[81] Nevertheless, the claim that these criteria were common to all legal systems laid the foundations for the development of uniform rules of Private International Law.

In the third place, it relied on *natural law*, if only to counteract the first and second tenets.[82] The principle that *statuta odiosa*, repugnant foreign laws, need not be applied by courts of other countries, drew upon general standards derived from reasoning outside the limited sphere of the domestic law of the court called upon to apply foreign law.

In the fourth place, if only in order to evade its own pitfalls, the statutist theory gave an opportunity to the parties to indicate a *choice of law*, either expressly or by implication, in a limited number of circumstances. It established the importance of choice of law by the parties.[83]

These four elements, the international, the universalistic, the ethical and the voluntaristic, have all contributed to the subsequent development of Private International Law.

Section 8. The French School in the 16th Century— Dumoulin and D'Argentré

12. The French school of the 16th century made its own contribution to the further refinement of the statutist doctrine, but its principal importance lies in the fact that it handled the technique of the statutists in a manner which prepared a later and entirely new approach. Its outstanding representatives, Dumoulin (1500-1566) [84] and D'Argentré (1519-1590),[85] showed highly individual, though opposing tendencies.[86] Dumoulin relied (though only in a limited number of cases) on the express or implied intention of the parties to select the law applicable. He is largely responsible for the introduction of the free choice of law into Private International Law.[87]

D'Argentré, under the influence of feudal ideas, expanded the range of rules which he regarded as *statuta realia* and restricted, correspondingly, the number of rules which, in his opinion, were to be treated as *statuta personalia*.[88] The French school of the 16th century, which was centred in the North, thus completed a development which had begun in the southern part of France in the late 13th and early 14th centuries. There Révigny and Belleperche had asserted the right of the local sovereign to enact special legislation overriding the *jus commune* and foreign law. D'Argentré pushed this development to a stage where the principles were reversed. If possible a statute is to be regarded as *realis*; only in exceptional circumstances is a personal character to be attributed to it. With the disappearance of the unilateral character of *statuta personalia* and *realia* this means no longer that every court must disregard foreign law and must apply the *lex fori*. Since the doctrine of *statuta personalia* and *realia* now covers foreign law as well, it means, in the great majority of cases, courts, wherever situate, must apply the *lex situs* on the ground that most rules of law are by their nature *statuta realia* designed to affect property and are by their nature restricted in space so as to operate only in the country in which they have been enacted. Yet neither Dumoulin nor D'Argentré abandoned the statutist doctrine as such, much as their own teachings suggested such a course. In particular, like the Italian, the French school failed to show why foreign laws, whether personal or real, could claim to be applied by courts outside the territory for which they had been enacted. The answer to this question was given by the Dutch writers of the 17th century.

Section 9. The Dutch School—Comity

13. With one notable exception, the Dutch school [89] of the late 17th century shows a strange discord. In all matters of practice Dutch writers adhered to the technique of the statutists, but they also showed another side. They were much exercised by the question why the courts of one country apply the laws of another country, be they personal or real. As shown above, this question had never been put either by the Italian or the French writers, who relied on the division of legislative powers as a principle of Private International Law, embodied originally in a rule of Roman law,[90] the universal validity of which was never questioned. Yet this problem was not merely a theoretical one. D'Argentré's attitude, which insisted that, with few exceptions, all statutes are real, had seriously undermined the universalistic approach to Private International Law. If most statutes purport only to operate within the territory of the legislature which enacted them, it becomes impossible to justify the application of those laws elsewhere by relying on the extra-territorial effect of personal statutes to which *statuta realia* formed an exception.[91] It must not be forgotten either, that the Dutch writers in the second half of the 17th century were acquainted with Bodin's [92] and Grotius' [93] works. These confirmed the division of legislative powers between States but did not bear out any specific duties of States to apply the laws of other countries in given circumstances. There was a division of legislative competence but no system of mutual enforcement of laws. The universalistic approach to Private International Law to the effect that foreign laws of a particular character apply everywhere by reason

of their nature had been refuted. There remained only a division of competence between States to legislate and a true conflict of laws. The application and enforcement of the law of other States, like all other international intercourse was determined by rules of international law.

An answer was attempted by P. Voet (1619-1677) when he said—

> "nonnunquam dum populus vicinus vicini mores *comiter* vult observare et ne multa bene gesta turbarentur, de moribus statuta territorium statuentis, inspecto effectu, solent egredi" [94]

and again—

> "statuta cuiuscunque sint generis, jus dicentis territorium neque propalam neque per consequentiam egredi. Nisi ex comitate. Ideo malui, id est tutius esse judicabam, ad solam humanitatem recurrere, qua populos vicinus vicini decreti comiter observat".[95]

His son Johannes (1647-1714) proclaimed the same principle:

> "de statutis personalibus non ita per generales regulas definiri potest, quousque alter alteriius, statuta ac decreta ex comitate servet".[96]

It is usual to credit Huber (1624-1694) with the presentation of the new doctrine of comity. While this is not strictly accurate, the credit must go to Huber for having combined the local doctrine of comity, which replaced the universalistic concept of Private International Law, with the international doctrine based upon a division of legislative competence. His doctrine is well expressed in the three maxims which restate the teachings of the Dutch school:

(1) The laws of every sovereign authority have force within the boundaries of its State and bind all subject to it, but not beyond.[97]
(2) Those are held to be subject to a sovereign authority who are found within the boundaries, whether they be there permanently or temporarily.[98]
(3) Those who exercise authority so act from comity that the laws of each nation which are enforced within its own boundaries should retain their effect, so far as they do not prejudice the power or rights of another State of its subjects.[99]

14. *The theoretical basis of Huber's doctrine.* The *international* basis of Huber's doctrine emerges from his first rule which proceeds from

the division of legislative competence among States and points to the jurisdiction of each State to legislate for its own subjects and in relation to its own territory. The *territorial* character of this legislative jurisdiction emerges from the second rule which limits the range of subjects to persons who are permanently or temporarily resident within the territory. The *local nature* of rules of Private International Law is set out in Huber's third rule. There are no principles of Private International Law which can claim universal validity.

The significance of the third rule is, however, obscured by Huber's reliance on comity. Doubts about its meaning have detracted from the effectiveness of the rule, a defect which was all the more serious since Huber's influence upon the development of English and American Private International Law was decisive. Taken as a minimum requirement it is equal to courtesy.[100] Taken as a maximum requirement it must be identical with legal duty.[101] Some help can be obtained from Huber himself in *Heedendaegse Rechtsgeleertheјt* [102] when he added, after formulating his three principles,

> "From this it is clear that the decision of such cases is part of the law of nations and not, properly speaking, of civil law, inasmuch as it does not depend on the individual pleasure of the higher powers of each country, but on the mutual convenience of the sovereign powers and their tacit agreement with each other".[103]

Thus according to Huber there was no duty arising by the nature of foreign private law to apply it (as the statutists assumed). Instead, customary international law (the tacit pact between States) [104] established a duty to give full effect to foreign law, *once a State has decided generally to apply foreign law in the particular circumstances.*

Put in another way, the stress laid on comity served to underline that foreign law need not be enforced as such and that no more than a general respect for foreign law, once chosen to apply in the particular circumstances of the case, was called for. Thus Huber may have envisaged a doctrine of acquired rights [105] for the limited purpose of countering the doctrine of the statutists rather than as the basis for establishing a duty to recognise private rights under customary international law.[106] Thus understood the respect postulated for foreign acquired rights may have served only as a motive for the consistent application of foreign law which would not apply *proprio motu*, as the statutists would have had it, but not as a principle requiring the application of foreign law as a matter of duty.[107]

15. Huber put his axioms into practice in his little treatise on the Conflict of Laws, as he aptly called the subject strictly in accordance with the legal situation as he saw it. In this treatise he abandons completely the statutist technique. The facts of the case are linked to one of several legal systems which may be applicable with the help of connecting factors such as domicile, place of contracting, place of performance, situs, place of action and the intention of the parties. For reasons which will be set out below it can pass as an introduction to Private International Law in England and in all countries which have adopted the common law. Nevertheless, as understood by Anglo-American writers and courts, Huber's doctrine was not entirely consistent. On the one hand it recognised the territoriality of laws based upon the international division of legislative competence and proclaimed an international custom to apply foreign territorial law which has operated in a particular instance. On the other hand, it rejected the statutist doctrine which determined the application of laws in space by reference to the nature of rules of law, but offered no substitute rules for determining when foreign law must be regarded as having operated territorially. Huber's treatise provided a number of examples with solutions showing the individual connecting factors, but no set of detailed independent rules of Private International Law. It was reasonably clear that, if all the facts arose within the legislative competence of country A, the courts of country B were to apply the law of A. If, however, the facts showed connections with several countries, the doctrine of territoriality as such, sanctioned by comity, could not provide a reliable guide for a choice of law. Instead, guidance had to be found, once again, *either* in tests chosen by any one system of municipal law according to its own notion of policy and justice *or* in tests chosen *a priori* upon the basis of certain fundamental principles alleged to be of international origin and validity.

The Dutch school gave birth to modern Private International Law. Special rules of the *lex fori*, and not the nature of domestic and foreign rules of private law determine whether municipal or foreign law must be applied. The question remained open, however, whether the Private International Law of the forum is strictly domestic law or whether it is *either* determined *or* controlled by Public International Law.

Section 10. The Subsequent Development of the Doctrine of Huber— England [108]

16. In its own time, the Dutch doctrine failed to gain adherents in continental Europe, where courts and writers remained faithful to the statutist doctrine up to the middle of the 19th century. It succeeded in England and in the United States, whence it returned to stimulate continental Private International Law. It could gain an easy foothold in England because the specific problems of Private International Law which had exercised the minds of lawyers in continental Europe for the last 500 years had not attracted much attention in England and because, when they did present themselves, English courts could approach them in accordance with the most recent Dutch technique, unfettered by the ballast of statutist learning which hindered progress abroad.

Until then, questions of choice of law had been sidestepped and had been answered without the help of rules of Private International Law. Either they were treated as questions of jurisdiction or they were solved by the application of a uniform system of laws deemed to be of universal application. If treated as questions of jurisdiction, and if English common law courts were competent, English law applied as a matter of course; if the English common law courts were not competent the case did not come up for trial at all in England. Alternatively, if the courts of Staple and Piedpowder, which heard disputes of foreign merchants in England, the Court of Admiralty, which exercised jurisdiction in cases arising on the high seas or abroad, or the courts of arbitration set up by the merchants themselves, assumed jurisdiction, they relied on the *Law Merchant* as a uniform system of universal application.[109] They never developed a system of choice of law.[110] It is true that earlier the Norman and the English part of the population had lived according to their personal law. It is also clear that in matters of distribution of personality, the ecclesiastical courts, which were charged with the administration of this branch of law in England, applied the law of the ecclesiastical province in which the accused had last resided, if the custom at the place of residence of the deceased and of the situs of the goods differed from each other.

Since English law was always applicable if the common law courts had jurisdiction, actions involving a foreign element only could not be tried in the absence of a venue in England. As in the Netherlands and Northern France in early feudal times,[111] jurisdiction and choice of law were closely connected. The contest was therefore an internal one between the jurisdiction of the common law courts and the Admiralty Court; indirectly it was between common law and law merchant, between English domestic law and uniform law, both of which were applicable in England. In the 18th century the attitude towards the exclusion of foreign law began to change. The common law courts began to apply the law merchant, first as a fact, and then as law. Lord Mansfield completed the process by incorporating the law merchant into English law. Thereby it lost its international and assumed a national character. Thus it became necessary to determine what law applied in cases involving a foreign element which were formerly decided according to the law merchant. This movement was assisted by other factors, among them the circumstance that foreign judgments had become enforceable in England (1607) and that the Privy Council now had occasion to hear cases from foreign possessions. Sitting as a court of appeal from a colonial court, it applied the local law as the law of the court. Throughout the first three-quarters of the 18th century cases were few,[112] and the reasons for applying foreign law were drawn from foreign writers.[113]

17. The general principle behind these cases which has inspired English Private International Law was formulated by Lord Mansfield in *Holman* v. *Johnson*:[114]

> "Every action here must be tried by the law of England, but the law of England says that in a variety of circumstances . . . the law of the country where the cause of action arose shall govern".[115]

Following Huber and the Dutch school, Lord Mansfield acknowledged that all laws are territorial and that it is for English law to determine whether and in what circumstances foreign law is to be applied in England. Having affirmed the local character of choice of law rules, Lord Mansfield's subsequent reference to the place of birth of the action abroad, while intended once more to emphasise the territorial character of law, introduced a static and undefined element inasmuch as it could be regarded as attributing a territorial character to a cause of action on the strength of an overriding division of territorial competences, and not on the basis of the Private International Law of the forum only. The Dutch school did not provide any general clues for ascertaining the place where a cause of action arises, and relied instead on connecting factors (such as domicile, place of contracting, place of performance, situs, etc.) freely adopted by the local choice of law rules. While these serve well the dual purpose of appearing as local rules and of pinpointing the territorial law where the cause of action arose, they cannot be said to fulfil necessarily both these tests if the situation or transaction in issue is centred in two or more countries. A marriage settlement made in one country by persons domiciled in two other countries whose property is situated in yet another provides such an example. Here the doctrine of territoriality does not provide an answer. It serves a useful purpose only as long as all the facts of a case arise in one country, while the action is brought in another. This ambiguity in Lord Mansfield's formulation was soon to lead to a new search for a general overriding principle which permitted to localise causes of action; otherwise a vicious circle might be perpetuated, for English law, which was said to refer to the law of the country where the cause of action arose, would itself have to define whether a cause of action arose abroad.[116]

The next 60 years witnessed only a slow growth in England of this new branch of the law. Few cases came before the courts; writers, too, were incapable of giving a lead, and the literature in England up to the middle of the 19th century was insignificant. The sterile statutist doctrines still held their own.[117]

Section 11. The United States

18. In the United States, the diversity of State legislation encouraged a vigorous interest in this new branch of the law.[118] Within the short period of 6 years three major works [119] appeared, one of which was of outstanding importance. Story's *Commentaries on the Conflict of Laws* was based on English and American law and on the writings of the French and Dutch schools. It was the first modern treatise on this subject, but on general principles Story had little to say, and what he said was not far removed from his Dutch forerunners. His maxims were these:

(1) "The first . . . maxim . . . is that every nation possesses an exclusive sovereignty and jurisdiction within its own territory. The direct consequence . . . is that the laws of every State affect and bind directly all property . . . within its territory, and all persons who are resident within it . . . and all contracts made and acts done within it." [120]

(2) "Another maxim . . . is that no State . . . can by its own law directly affect or bind property out of its own territory or bind persons not resident therein . . . it would be . . . incompatible with . . . the sovereignty of all nations that one nation should be at liberty to regulate either persons or things not within its own territory." [121]

(3) "From these two maxims ... flows a third ... that whatever force ... the laws of one country have in another depends solely upon the laws ... of the latter ... upon its own express or tacit consent." [122]

This statement of principle comes very near to that of Huber, but Story's maxims are both fuller and more precise. The first maxim combines Huber's first and second principles. It expresses the international principle of territoriality in respect of persons, objects and acts. The second maxim has no counterpart in Huber's work. It rejects the statutist doctrine of the extra-territoriality of *statuta personalia*. The third reduces the doctrine of comity from an international duty to a domestic motive. There is no duty imposed by customary international law to apply foreign law. Private International Law is domestic law unfettered by any external rules. The era of 19th-century Private International Law had arrived.[123]

However, while this principle provides an acceptable working basis for conflicts of laws involving several independent countries, it may be that Story, a Federal Judge, failed to give sufficient attention to the specific problems which can arise in the United States, a Federal State, where private law is not uniform. Here the insight that Private International Law is municipal law unfettered by overriding principles of international law may be counterbalanced by the requirements of the Constitution. This specifically American problem has since been presented by recent American writers as 20th-century Private International Law.[124]

Section 12. Modern Private International Law—Wächter, Savigny

19. The success of Story's work in England and on the Continent of Europe, where the statutist doctrine had lingered on, was immediate.[125] The French Civil Code of 1804 does not follow any particular doctrine of Private International Law, and it is a matter of doubt whether it adopted the statutist or the Dutch doctrine,[126] while the Austrian provisions in the Code of 1811 are regarded as statutist in conception.[127] In Germany, Wächter, in a thought-provoking article, reviewed the development of the conflict of laws in that country.[128] He was able to show that in the 17th and 18th centuries the classical doctrine of the statutists had been attacked by German writers [129] on the ground that it was "ill-defined, capable of different meanings, uncertain and varying" [130] and had been modified in its fundamentals.[131] Even if laws are territorial, it is not the duty of other countries to follow them,[132] no matter whether

the territorial law is the *lex domicilii* [133] or the *lex situs*.[134] Moreover, the fact that a foreign country is competent according to international law to legislate within its own territory, does not prove that such country necessarily desires to subject every person and every object within it to its own laws,[135] and it may well be that it wishes to exclude them from their operation. The doctrine of acquired rights does not provide a solution since its only effect is to prohibit retroactive legislation.[136] If the doctrine of acquired rights, understood in a wider, territorial sense, were correct, every country would be obliged to pay unlimited respect to the laws of other countries, where such rights are alleged to have arisen, but such a submission to foreign law had never been asserted even by its protagonists.[137] The true purpose of the doctrine of acquired rights as a motive for the adoption of some choice of law rules and not as a legal precept requiring the application of foreign law in particular circumstances defined by some overriding legal principles had even been admitted by one of its exponents.[138] Wächter thus perceived that neither the claim of foreign law to apply (as the statutists believed) nor their foreign territorial character (as some supporters of the Dutch school thought) offered a guide for the court seized with the dispute. Such a court was faced with the determination of a—

> "legal relationship which had either its origin abroad or in which foreigners participated or which otherwise has contacts abroad".[139]

From this he concluded: the court must follow its own domestic law [140] unless the statute law of the forum provides definite criteria for exercising a choice of law [141] or (it would seem) unless the common law contains choice of law rules [142] or spatially conditioned rules.[143] In advocating a solution which pays particular regard to the limitations in space of the substantive rules of private law of the *forum*, Wächter took a dangerous step backwards towards the early practice of the post-glossators; especially by insisting that the *lex fori* must be applied always, if it is mandatory in character *(jus cogens)* [144] he fell back on the learning of the statutists.[145] Finally, it was difficult to proclaim the existence of a general overriding principle, if it is the task of the parties to prove foreign law and not of the court to find it *proprio motu*.[146]

20. The credit for having shown a new approach goes normally to Savigny,[147] but in the main arguments he was preceded by Wächter. Savigny, too, refused to determine the application of laws in space in virtue of the nature of such laws; [148] he, too, refused to attach any im-

portance to the alleged territoriality of laws [149] on the ground, firstly, that no one territory alone is normally involved and, secondly, that the doctrine of acquired rights is fallacious.[150] Both Wächter and Savigny offered a new solution. The legal relationship before the court was the starting point. The court must determine what law applies. At this stage, however, the two scholars parted company. Wächter relied on the rules of domestic and conflict of laws of the forum.[151] Savigny believed that the rules of conflict of laws were of universal application based on the—

> "international community of nations in interchange with each other".[152]

The test was simple. He believed that—

> "for each legal relationship that legal system must be ascertained to which this legal relationship pertains or is subject having regard to its particular nature".[153]

The legal relationship and its seat were thus made the elements of all rules of Private International Law. It was only necessary to give formal expression to the tests (now known as connecting factors) according to which the seat was determined by the community of nations.

The number of legal relationships which require to be connected with a particular system of laws is of course infinite, and it may be, as will be shown below, that an almost infinite choice of law or spatially conditioned choice of law rules can and should be ascertained and developed. However, ever since Huber had written his account of the conflict of laws it was clear that for the purpose of the latter legal relationships had been reduced to a limited number of typical situations which relate to the person, property, contract, tort, succession and a small number of others.[154] Each of these can be attributed a centre at a place which can be determined with some certainty: domicile, residence, situs, place of contracting, place of performance, place where an act has been completed and so on. These tests are now known as connecting factors. Savigny believed that they were of universal application. Story and Wächter, whose opinion turned out to be right, thought that they were not, but differed from country to country.[155]

21. At first sight it might seem that Wächter and Savigny halted halfway when they made the legal relationship the starting point. It might even be argued that the statutist notion according to which all laws are personal or real had been transposed into the individual case;

all legal situations have a personal, proprietary, contractual or delictual character, or they fall within the realm of succession or procedure. It might be objected that legal relationships exist only in virtue of some system of laws and that an attempt to ascertain the law applicable to a particular situation by linking a legal relationship to a legal system which is to apply to it anticipates the choice of law.[156] Ideally only a set of facts can be connected with a legal system before it can be stated that a legal relationship exists. In reality no pure factual situation before the court induces a choice of law. The need to determine whether foreign, rather than domestic, law must be applied arises in practice if the plaintiff frames his claim or the defendant his reply according to some foreign law. Foreign law is not selected in the abstract but only in respect of a particular claim or defence. Thus the legal relationship is rightly treated as the object on which the rules of Private International Law operate. This conclusion opens up a new problem. Since legal relationships in the *abstract* form the principal element of domestic choice of law rules, which connect these relationstips with a particular system of laws with the help of connecting factors, and since the object of the dispute is a *concrete* legal relationship expressed in the form of a claim or defence, the integration of the concrete relationship into the abstract relationship formulated in the choice of rule causes a problem of interpretation which is known as characterization, or qualification.[157]

Whatever new problems came into being with it, the modern technique of handling questions of Private International Law had emerged.[158] Immediately following its birth, however, the search began again for some overriding firm principles which could determine when the forum should apply its own or foreign law.

Section 13. Modern Doctrines of Territoriality or Pseudo-Territoriality —Acquired Rights

22. The teachings of Story and Savigny exercised much influence upon Westlake [159] and Dicey [160] in England whose practical, empirical approach was in sympathy with them. The legal basis of the English conflict of laws remained Lord Mansfield's pronouncement in *Holman* v. *Johnson* [161] to the effect that English rules of the conflict of laws, as part of English domestic law, refer to foreign law in certain circumstances. Dicey never waivered in his adherence to this rule of English law.[162] However, he supplemented his firm belief in the local character of choice of law rules by an express reliance on the doctrine of acquired

rights.[163] This doctrine is of some antiquity and can be traced to the postglossators,[164] though it is doubtful whether they wished to apply it to questions of the conflict of laws.[165] In juxtaposition with the common law rule expressed in *Holman* v. *Johnson,*[166] the principle of the protection of acquired rights makes little sense and is open to the charge of circuity. It has been refuted again and again by eminent writers who have shown that since rights exist only in virtue of some system of laws, the protection of foreign acquired rights assumes that foreign law has been applied; thus Private International Law which, it is said, must respect foreign acquired rights, must first determine by its own rules of the conflict of laws whether a right has been acquired.[167]

The researches of Nadelmann have traced the development of this idea by Dicey.[168] He acknowledged his indebtedness to Holland, whose *Elements of Jurisprudence* included the statement that the conflict of laws deals in reality with the recognition of rights created and defined by foreign law.[169] It is difficult to see how Holland reached this conclusion for his reference to Vattel is spurious and that to Wächter reverses the latter's thoughts.[170] It is possible that Holland derived it from Huber [171] whom he cited in the second edition of his work.

There are indications that Dicey was aware of the limited function of the doctrine of acquired rights in Huber's system when he qualified his principle by stating:

> "The word 'duly' [acquired] . . . fixes in effect the limit of the application of General Principle I. This principle is . . . only that rights which have been *in the opinion of English courts* [italics mine] properly and rightly acquired are . . . enforceable here." [172]

Thus understood the doctrine of acquired rights does not suffer from the flaws expressed by its critics, limited as it is to providing a motive or explanation for applying foreign law and for applying it consistently, once chosen, but it has also become meaningless as a theory. Nevertheless a doctrine of acquired rights in the sense considered here may support the object of rules of Private International Law and may claim some practical merits which may have influenced Dicey when he said:

> ". . . the principle of the enforcement of vested rights does not supply such a universal test. To admit this, however, is quite consistent with maintaining that this principle does define the object in the main aimed at by rules having reference to the conflict of laws or to the extra-territorial effect of rights." [173]

The court, in England at least, is invited, not to ascertain and to apply foreign law of its own motion when faced with a factual statement of claim, but to decide whether a claim brought in the light of some legal system [174] can be sustained. It is for the parties to submit a claim based on some legal system, and it is for the court in England to determine whether the claim as framed according to some foreign law is framed in accordance with that legal system which applies according to the English rules of the conflict of laws.[175] In the end, a choice must be made, and it must be made in accordance with English Private International Law, but the initiative lies with the parties who submit claims, counterclaims and defences which rely not merely on facts but combine facts with reliance on some foreign system of laws. Technically this insight may prove useful in many respects, as will be shown later on in connection with the discussion of characterisation and *renvoi*. If this was Dicey's view, his juxtaposition of a system of domestic rules of the conflict of laws, unfettered by any overriding considerations or principles, and of a doctrine of acquired rights is not inconsistent. The former provides the legal basis; the latter serves to explain a technical device.

23. An additional practical observation is appropriate here. Private International Law is not exclusively concerned with the enforcement of rights by way of judicial process; it also serves to instruct the parties who are about to conclude some transaction, such as marriage or contract, whether to comply with the rules of this or that system of laws.[176] Any doctrine that Private International Law is exclusively concerned with the protection of foreign acquired rights would only be justifiable on one of two assumptions:

The first alternative assumption is that an international system of conflict of laws determines in what circumstances foreign law must be applied. In this case local courts would only be called upon to enforce rights which had been brought into existence by a legal system operating with universal effect. However, no such system exists in the international sphere; within a Federal State an overriding system of federal conflict of laws can provide such a framework, though no such system is believed to exist at the present time.[177a] At best, the experience in the United States shows that the law of a particular State can or cannot apply in the presence or absence of a clear connection with the State concerned.[177]

The second alternative assumption is that a strict system of territoriality exists coupled with the duty to enforce foreign rights which had come into being in accordance with the territorial laws of the particular country. The first part of this hypothetical principle formed the substance of the Dutch doctrine. As was shown above, only a small number of situations involving a foreign element arise exclusively within the confines of one particular territorial system of laws and, secondly, that legal system does not necessarily wish to apply to the case in question. The second part of the hypothetical rule involves the question, also raised by the Dutch doctrine, whether foreign law which operates territorially must be applied by the courts in other countries as a matter of legal obligation of an international character, or whether the choice of law is a matter for the *lex fori,* in deference to its own sense of policy and convenience.[178] As will be shown later on [179] there are no overriding rules of international law which force one country to *apply* the territorial law of another country, even if the entire factual situation is centred in the latter. It follows that the duty to apply foreign law on the ground that the cause of action arose within the legislative competence of a particular foreign country can only be found in some provision of the domestic law of the *forum.* The legal system which purports to protect rights which were acquired in a foreign country must first bring these rights into being.

24. A doctrine of Private International Law which is based upon a doctrine of territorially acquired rights and which avoids the pitfalls of a vicious circle must therefore assume that all causes of action are necessarily centred within the territory of one country only and that foreign law which has operated territorially must be applied everywhere if the cause of action arose within its legislative competence.

Such a doctrine was supplied by Beale [180] and through him inspired the First Restatement of the Conflict of Laws. In the first place, he overcame the difficulty that in most cases involving a foreign element the cause of action does not arise exclusively in one country by relying on tests selected arbitrarily upon *a priori* considerations.[181] In the second place, he identified the duty to apply the law of the foreign country with the duty to respect foreign sovereignty. The fallacy of this reasoning is clear[182] if it is remembered, first, that the cause of action is initially located in the foreign country by the application of *a priori* principles provided by the author himself and, second, that the wish or disinclination of the foreign sovereign to determine the cause of action by his own laws is never considered. The *forum* is first made to confer legislative competence upon the foreign sovereign and is then employed to determine the material exercise of those powers. Nevertheless, as was indicated above [183] and will be shown below,[184] such a doctrine embodying a distribution and mutual respect of territorial legislative powers may be useful in controlling the ambit and the application of choice of law rules in a Federal State, such as the United States, where a maximum of respect is due to the law of Member States.[185]

25. In the period between the two World Wars, the pendulum in the United States has swung in the opposite direction. Where formerly the doctrine of the territoriality of laws and of the protection of acquired rights had been most firmly entrenched, several new schools of thought took its place. It was the merit of Lorenzen to have led the way towards the dethronement of Beale's doctrine of acquired rights together with the dogmatic tests linking certain types of legal relations (operative facts) with particular countries or territories.[186] Thus Private International Law, especially in the Anglo-American world, reached its full maturity, a part of domestic law unfettered by any shackles, except those which Public International Law imposed upon domestic law in general.[187]

Proceeding from the same basis as Lorenzen, the "local law" theory [188] put forward by W. W. Cook asserts that the forum neither applies foreign law nor enforces foreign acquired rights, but rights created by the *lex fori* in a form which approximates as closely as possible to similar rights abroad. In the words of W. W. Cook:

> "The forum, when confronted by a case involving foreign elements, always applies its own law to the case, but in doing so adopts and enforces as its own law a rule of decision identical, or at least highly similar, though not identical, in scope with a rule of decision found in the system of law in force in another state [189] with which some or all of the foreign elements are connected . . . The rule thus 'incorporated' into the law of the forum . . . the forum . . . enforces not a foreign right but a right created by its own law." [190]

In so far as Cook denied that *a priori* considerations lead to the location of a cause of action or right in a foreign country and that such rights must be recognised or enforced elsewhere, he accomplished the same task as Lorenzen. The attempt to substitute "locally created rights" for the vanished "foreign created rights" adds no new insight, once it is accepted with Lorenzen that Private International Law is unadulterated domestic law. It adds no new insight into the question why foreign law is applied, though it does seek to explain how it is applied.

26. The manner in which foreign law is introduced into the law of the forum has occupied writers, especially in Italy, who found it difficult to reconcile the notion that the forum is exclusively subject to its own law with the postulate that the former may have to apply law which is foreign in origin. Doctrines of incorporation, such as those of the *rinvio ricettizio o materiale* [191] or the adoption of "special" rules of domestic law side by side with those of domestic law proper,[192] have sought to provide a solution to a problem which has little practical importance.[193]

27. In the light of this evaluation of the local law theory it is unnecessary to examine the contention that in reality two separate local law theories have been expounded.[194] It must suffice to indicate that the local law doctrine adopted by Learned Hand in the District Court for the Southern District of New York and in the Circuit Court of Appeals [195] may be less radical. According to the latter, a right must have come into existence within the legislative competence of a foreign territorial sovereign in accordance with *a priori* considerations suggested by Beale, but the enforcement of such a right is not a legal duty incumbent upon other countries as a legal duty. Instead they grant relief which is as nearly as possible identical with the right created abroad. Thus Learned Hand J. may have accepted the doctrine of the territoriality of laws but rejected the duty to respect foreign acquired rights or foreign sovereignty. In so doing he may have expounded a local law doctrine of a second degree. In the search for an answer to the question why foreign law is to be applied and whether any specific rules outside the discretion of the *lex fori* determine the choice, the local law doctrine does not assist. It affirms that Private International Law is part of domestic law and is determined by the traditions and policies inherent in the latter.

Section 14. Sociological Neo-Statutists

28. During the second half of the 19th century and during the early part of the 20th century, codifications of Private International Law in Europe and elsewhere, except in common law countries and in Scandinavia, were much influenced by the sociological approach of Man-

cini.[196] It centres on nations, as shaped by territory, race, language, custom, history, laws and religion as the nuclei of modern international organisation. The link between the individual and a particular nucleus is not created by residence within one nation but by the tie of allegiance created by the possession of a given nationality; permanent residence and nationality may not coincide [197] but, unlike in the common law,[198] civil and political status are both determined by the same criterion. Accordingly the *lex patriae* applies, but if "voluntary" as distinct from "necessary" private law is involved the *lex patriae* may give way to another system of laws to be selected by the parties. Whether a law is "necessary" or "voluntary" depends upon the nature of the rule of law concerned. More specifically it depends upon whether the rule is an expression of the special characteristics of the nation composing the State by which it was created. These characteristics are said to make themselves felt most strongly in the law relating to status, capacity, family relations and succession. Finally local rules which bear the character of public policy,[199] especially those affecting property within the jurisdiction, have an overriding effect.

Thus, the statutist notion of the nature of laws determining their operation in space and the criterion of the "but social" [200] are called in aid to establish fixed principles which determine, indirectly through the connecting factors nationality and situs, which law is to apply or whether free choice is allowed. In the different climate of the United States a similar cord was struck by Currie.[201]

Others, similarly bent on developing a system of international application, relied on the notion of sovereignty. On the assumption that sovereignty extends over all property within its sway, and over all nationals within and without the territorial reach, it is asserted that the *lex patriae* governs all matters affecting persons and that the *lex situs* governs all matters concerning things.[202] It is only one further step to assert that the *lex patriae* and the *lex situs* are the only two systems of law to which the Private International Law of the forum may refer. In face of the fact that the world's systems of Private International Law have developed different and more sophisticated connecting factors, it is admitted that the *lex patriae* and the *lex situs* themselves can, by their own rules of Private International Law, refer to other systems of law with the help of such connecting factors as domicile, residence, place of contracting and place of performance. Thus the Private International Law of the forum is severely restricted in its choice, the emphasis is shifted to the Private International Law of the *lex causae* and *renvoi* is elevated to a position of paramount importance. In effect every country could, and probably would, provide two systems of Private International Law. One would apply to foreign nationals and to objects situated abroad and would be bound to rely solely on the *lex patriae* and the *lex situs*; the other, much more differentiated and unfettered, using other connecting factors, could apply to its own nationals and to all objects situate within its own jurisdiction.

Section 15. Wächter redivivus—Ehrenzweig

29. In a series of consecutive studies [203] culminating in three major works, Ehrenzweig [204] has mounted a frontal attack against what he alleges is the present tendency towards conceptualism, internationalism and a mechanical application of foreign law regardless of the practical realities. In its latest formulation he puts forward seven propositions: [205]

Firstly, choice of law is a matter for the law of the forum, unfettered by any overriding principle except treaties or, in a Federal State, overriding rules of the Constitution;[206]

secondly, where no specific or emerging choice of law rule can be identified in practice, the question whether foreign law applies must be determined by references to the substantive rule of law of the forum, which must be interpreted as regards its claim to apply in space;[207]

thirdly, the interpretation of the substantive rules of the forum often results in their own application even in respect of situations involving a foreign element;[208]

fourthly, if no choice of law rule, either express or implied by the process of interpretation set out above, which leads to the application of foreign law can be isolated, the substantive rule of the forum applies as a residuary law;[209]

fifthly, the *lex fori* applies to questions of procedure, rules of factual interpretation,[210] standards of behaviour such as negligence, public policy and by virtue of an agreement to this effect by the parties;[211]

sixthly, the recognition of the existence of certain rules of foreign law does not necessarily indicate that a choice of law rule of the forum has given it effect;[212]

seventhly, existing choice of law rules often operate subject to considerable modifications in practice brought about by judicial interpretation, the characterisation of the operative facts, the circumstance that the *lex fori* and the *lex causae* are identical in substance or, while differing in substance, lead to identical results.[213]

Finally, the operation of choice of law rules is limited, as a matter of policy, by the "principle of validation" and the respect for the autonomous choice of law by the parties.[214]

Of these propositions, the first four concern the basis of Private International Law. The principal tenets are not new; they reproduce Wächter's notions [215] that primarily established choice of law rules and spatially conditioned rules of the forum must provide guidance and that, failing such rules, the substantive law of the forum applies. The advance beyond Wächter lies in the second proposition which emphasises the role played by the interpretation of the substantive rule of the forum in order to determine its operation in space. The assumption is that the interpretation of a rule of substantive law can yield an answer to the question whether it applies within the territory of the forum or also beyond. Such an assumption was made by the statutists, whose tests, namely whether the law affected persons or things, proved unworkable.[216] It may be that modern interpretation seeking to ascertain the purpose of a rule [217] can succeed where the postglossators failed. Yet several lacunae remain. In interpreting a rule of domestic substantive law it may be possible to read into it a spatially conditioned rule, or a unilateral choice of law rule, but not a bilateral rule. Thus it would only be possible to ascertain whether the substantive rule of the *lex fori* applies or not; if it does not apply, the question remains whether the case is to be dismissed, or whether some rule of foreign law applies in virtue of a choice of law rule which is to be found extraneously of the rule of domestic substantive law. In the former case, jurisdiction and choice of law are made to coincide; in the latter case, the system of Ehrenzweig is less far reaching than it seems. Ehrenzweig himself realised that in giving preponderance to the substantive law of the *forum*, the choice of jurisdiction assumes overriding importance and that rules of jurisdiction must be devised which exclude manipulations of the choice of law by an easy access to the local courts.[218] If, therefore, rules of jurisdiction are to be formulated which, through the identity of jurisdiction and choice of law, result in the application of what appears to be desirable rule of law, such rules of jurisdiction must embody those rules which formerly determined the desired choice of law. Thus the problem of choice of law continues to exist; only it has been transposed and becomes a problem of jurisdiction. Such a system, which was described above [219] existed in the middle ages in Northern France and in the Netherlands.

It has left its imprint in English Private International Law, especially in the sphere of status and of title to immovable property and in certain provisions relating to assumed jurisdiction,[220] until the rigidity of the older jurisdictional rules was relaxed. Its merits are simplicity and the reduced need to apply foreign law. Its defect is not only the denial of a remedy but also of a court if the narrow jurisdictional requirements cannot be met.

The attempt to attach choice of law rules to individual substantive rules of the *lex fori* opens up interesting prospects, despite the shortcomings inherent in Ehrenzweig's present exposition. As an alternative to the present technique which relies on broad choice of law rules [221] it merits attention for its subtlety and flexibility, provided that the choice of law is not conceived in unilateral terms only.

30. By relying on the continental approach which starts from the local rules of the conflict of laws and by stressing the need to connect the individual rule of substantive law with the legal system to be applied, this doctrine from the United States follows traditional lines of thinking in this field. It must be noted, however, that the propositions set out above allow a special reservation for overriding rules of public international and constitutional law. The former, more general problem will be discussed later on.[222] The latter, which is confined to the United States where it has influenced much modern thought purporting to be of universal validity, must be set out here, before it is possible to consider the most recent doctrines emanating from the North American continent.

Section 16. Conflict of Laws and the American Constitution

31. For the present purpose, which is to determine whether any overriding rules of the conflict of laws can be discovered in the constitutional law of the United States [223] it is unnecessary to examine the history and aims of the various provisions of the Constitution of the United States which affect the choice of law by State and Federal courts,[224] their development following the changing tendencies of the Supreme Court of the United States to curtail or to encourage the vigorous growth of local legislation and its effective exercise, or the emergence of the rule that there is no federal common law and therefore no federal conflict of laws to be administered in the Federal courts.[225] It must be stressed, however, that even if after the decision in *Klaxon* v. *Stentor* [226] the

common law is not the law common to the Federation, but applies with variants, and modified by local legislation, as separate systems of law in the Member States, nevertheless the common core has remained such that in most matters of private law conflicts arise principally because legislative measures in some States have modified the rules of the common law, especially in matters of contract and tort.

One conclusion is clear. The Supreme Court of the United States cannot determine the applicable law,[227] given that, subject to the Constitution, the Member States are sovereign and stand to each other in a relationship governed by international law.[228] The respect for the territorial competence of Member States in legislative and judicial matters furnishes the basis of this relationship.

> "Prima facie every State is entitled to enforce in its own courts its own laws, unless . . ." [229]

This guarantee of independence in legislative and judicial matters is matched by that accorded to other Member States. As a result conflicting overlaps [230] or cumulative abstentions [231] may occur. At first the Fourteenth Amendment served to protect rights acquired on the strength of foreign territorial jurisdiction,[232] but in due course the Full Faith and Credit Clause which secured the enforcement of judgments given by a court of a Member State, if competent according to the principles of the Constitution, was called in aid to safeguard the application of the substantive law of a Member State.[233] Thus a basic conflict could arise between—

> "the strong unifying principle embodied in the Full Faith and Credit Clause looking towards maximum enforcement in each state of the obligations or rights created or recognized by the statutes of sister states . . . and the policy of [the forum]".[234]

This conflict is not to be solved by supplanting the *lex fori* by foreign law every time that a sister State has acted within its competence and by obliging the courts of the forum in these circumstances always to apply law other than its own [235] to persons and events within the *forum*,[236]

> ". . . the full faith and credit clause does not require one state to substitute for its own statute, applicable to persons and events within it, the conflicting statute of another state, even though that statute is of controlling force in the courts of the state of its enactment with regard to the same persons and events",

even if the law of the sister State is of controlling force in the latter State in respect of the same persons and events.[237]

> "The purpose of the Full Faith and Credit Clause was to alter the status of the several states as independent sovereignties, each free to ignore obligations created under the laws ... of the others, and to make them integral parts of a single nation throughout which a remedy upon a just application might be demanded as of right, irrespective of the state of origin. That purpose ought not lightly to be set aside out of deference to a local policy ..." [238]

It is necessary to balance the claims of the competing laws to apply:

> "... but the room left for the play of conflicting policies is a narrow one ... For the States of the Union the constitutional limitation imposed by the Full Faith and Credit clause abolished in large measure the general principle of international law by which local policy is permitted to dominate rules of comity." [239]

In a series of decisions the balance has been struck by the test which focuses on the interest of the States concerned [240] and—

> "by appraising the governmental interests of each jurisdiction and turning the scale of decision according to their weight".[241]

In striking the balance, it is accepted that the forum has power to determine its own affairs and may disregard claims based on the law of a Member State which otherwise merit recognition and enforcement,[242] not merely if its own policy is different, but if the law of the sister State is clearly contrary to the public policy of the forum.[243]

It is clear that the absence of any contact between the relationship upon which the claim is based and the forum precludes the *lex fori* from being applied on the sole ground that one of the parties to the relationship is a citizen.[244] The relationship itself furnishes the criterion, and it is relevant whether it existed before the cause of action arose (such as a contract) or whether it came into being at the same time as the cause of action (such as a tort).[245] As regards contracts the protection of acquired rights has even been put forward as a restrictive test or motive.[246] Yet the *lex loci delicti* has been allowed to apply rather than the *lex contractus*, and the *lex fori* rather than the *lex loci delicti*.[247] In giving licence to the *lex fori* in preference to some other law, it matters whether the plaintiff can effectively sue the defendant elsewhere.[248] In maintaining the application of the law of a sister State it matters whether that law affords the defendant a defence of which he would be deprived if the *lex fori* applied.[249]

While it might have been possible to argue at the outset that in "appraising the governmental interests of each jurisdiction",[250] the Supreme Court of the United States proposed to examine the grouping of the connecting factors [251] so as to determine which Government is principally involved and to ascertain the seat of the relationship, thus replacing Story by Savigny, the subsequent development has shown that the court seeks to establish no more by this process than to strike a balance between the claims of the various jurisdictions and to safeguard justice between party and party in a very limited number of factual situations [252] by analysing the rules of law in issue. Not unnaturally the problems which beset the statutists reappeared arising out of modern legislation and couched in the technical language of today.[253] Once again an attempt was made to rely on the notion of territoriality of laws, now presented in terms of federal constitutional law as one of legislative jurisdiction. Once again it proved impossible, in situations which show local contact with several territorial units or legislative jurisdictions, to state with certainty that the relationship or cause of action has arisen in any one individual territory. Unable to rely on fixed rules of Private International Law, be they only of the dogmatic nature provided by Beale, the Supreme Court of the United States fell back on principles which attempt to determine the application of law in space through an analysis of the nature of the law in issue and of its claim to apply within its own territory or also without. Yet a Federal Supreme Court may succeed where the statutists failed because neither the writers themselves nor the courts which they served could claim overriding authority. Unable to determine in individual cases with contacts in several States of the Union which territorial sovereignty and therefore which legislative jurisdiction was involved, the Supreme Court seeks to reach the same determination by considering the aims and consequences of the rules put forward respectively by the parties. The selection of the proper legislative jurisdiction is achieved by an analysis or evaluation of the rules themselves. It is not surprising, therefore, that the most recent doctrine in the United States has taken as its themes the two general guide-lines which the Supreme Court has established for itself in order to carry out its duties under the Constitution—appraising governmental interests involved—justice between the parties—and has sought to give them a new life as general principles of universal application for determining the purpose and limitations of Private International Law or the Conflict of Laws.

32. These doctrines do not seek to develop and refine the principles which the Supreme Court of the United States has followed in controlling the choice of law rules forming part of the law of the Member States in order to ensure their compliance with the overriding principles of the Constitution which were analysed above. Undoubtedly the new doctrines did not exclude this goal in their general purpose which was to provide the courts of the Member States in the Federation with rules of general validity capable, incidentally, of serving as rules of universal application in other countries not subject to a federal system. In the ensuing discussion the distinction between these two separate uses must be constantly borne in mind.

Section 17. Governmental Interests as Conflict Resolving Factors—Currie—Neo-statutists

33. The first of these two doctrines seeks to determine the application of law in space by analysing the governmental interests underlying the rules of law which are said to conflict. It is connected with the name of Brainerd Currie.[254] It rejects orthodox rules of the conflict of laws which are part of the *lex fori* and refer the forum to foreign law in particular situations. It is obvious, however, that not all available legal systems and their rules can or may be scrutinised in order to ascertain their governmental interest to apply.

The question must be put why the rules of law of some legal systems can be examined for the purpose of determining the governmental interests involved, while others are not. Two possibilities exist. Either the consideration of rules of law belonging to foreign legal systems is determined by the *lex fori* or by overriding principles. The answer is not made any easier if it is realised that the new system is evolved exclusively from conflicts of law in matters of tort and contract, limited, moreover, to conflict of laws in the United States. Here the *lex fori*, the *lex actus*, the *lex injuriae* and the law of the respective home countries of the parties as well as the *lex loci solutionis* offer a baffling plethora of choice. At the same time all those laws originate in territorial units and, unlike rules of law selected by a free choice of law, can be regarded as claiming to be applied either generally within their own area, or with limitations only, or to extend to persons and events abroad. The assertion of the doctrine that it examines all governmental interests concerned seems to point to the conclusion that rules forming part of these various legal systems are taken into account because Member States of the United States must respect the sovereign powers of other Member States. If this is the case, the choice of law is determined in the first instance by considerations of American Constitutional Law, which does not contain, and cannot easily admit, fixed rules of conflict of laws and requires respect for the law of other Member States. The doctrine would, in these circumstances, be primarily national, and its value internationally must form the object of a special examination.

It must be admitted, however, that in looking to the legal systems of the restricted range of jurisdictions, this doctrine starts from the premise that a choice of law is primarily entrusted to the *lex fori*, but that in evolving sophisticated rules which may play fast and loose with orthodox choice of law rules, the autonomy of the *lex fori* must be reconciled with the claims of other States to see their law applied. Although such an interpretation starts from a premise which is the opposite to that examined before, it ends, once again, in according priority to aspects of American Constitutional Law. The only difference is that according to the first interpretation, an overriding system of the conflict of laws is emerging; according to the second interpretation, the limits of free choice of law are explored. In attempting to solve the question which of these two approaches inspires Currie's doctrine, some insight can be obtained from the stress which is laid on what it calls "false conflicts". Although it is not easy to determine all the facets of this new notion,[255] it seems to be agreed that a case presents a false conflict if either the rules of law of the various legal systems concerned are the same or, if they should differ in content, nevertheless produce the same result or do not purport to apply. It would seem that in practice, parties to a dispute do not plead the different rules in such circumstances, and no conflict of laws arises. The situation assumes another complexion if an overriding principle, which may be in the nature of constitutional law, requires imperatively that a selection must be made. Such would appear to be the assumption made by the adherents of the doctrine of governmental interests.

34. Whichever view is adopted, when it comes to determine the governmental interests involved in particular rules belonging to different legal systems, it is well to remember the experience gained in previous centuries that rules of substantive law can, but do not usually, indicate

their claim to be applied extensively or restrictively in space. When they do, it is possible to respect this wish.[256] When they do not, attempts to ascertain the application of rules in space by reference to the nature of the rules themselves, such as those made by the statutists, have failed. The doctrine which is associated with Currie may not seek directly to determine the claim to apply in space and its limits, but in seeking to unearth the respective unexpressed governmental interests underlying the rules concerned in order to allow one of these to prevail over another [257] it does so indirectly. Nor can it be expected that such an assessment of foreign governmental interests can be reached on objective rather than subjective grounds. Wächter's observations, put forward in reply to the alleged duty to respect foreign acquired rights because the respect for the foreign territorial sovereign demanded it, must be recalled here: the courts in one country are incapable of determining whether in the view of another country the latter's sovereignty (or, as it might be said in the present context, its interests) are affected and, if so, to what extent.[258] Any attempt to determine such interests must remain an exercise by the courts of the *forum* in interpreting foreign law, and the various explanations given to the relevant Ontario law on claims by guest passengers in order to support the decision in *Babcock* v. *Jackson* [259] bear out this contention. The task may not seem to be insuperable in the United States, where the differences in the law of tort and contract of the Member States are represented by legislation which modifies, enlarges, restricts, and generally improves the rules of the common law which forms the basis in all but one of the States. It assumes an entirely different dimension, if the rules in question are drawn from the common law, civil law in the form of different codifications, and Germanic law. The novelty of this doctrine is its exclusive reliance on unilateral rules of conflict of laws or on spatially conditioned rules. Failing any express guidance by such rules, their absence is replaced by an interpretation of the substantive rules of law. However, substantive law cannot be translated into spatially conditioned rules without doing violence to the rules of substantive law themselves and without the use of artificial devices.

Moreover, the doctrine assumes that legal systems wish to restrict or to extend their application in general and of individual rules in particular to certain areas or classes of persons. It remains to be examined later on whether such an analysis is universally valid or whether it is restricted to the special conditions of a Federal State.[260] It must be pointed out at this stage, however, that in the international sphere individual legal systems may perhaps be regarded as closed and self-sufficient, subject only to express limitations imposed by their own law.

Section 18. "Result Selecting" Principles—Cavers

35. After a long period when the protagonist of the "result selecting" doctrine, Cavers, was regarded in company with others [261] as a disciple of Aldricus [262] who favoured the application of the "better law" in the individual case, it is now clear that this doctrine seeks to establish new choice of law principles and does not renounce upon them altogether.[263] The existing rules are taken for granted.[264] Only when the need arises to fill gaps, the old technique is to be abandoned either to subsume the new problem under the established categories of choice of law rules or to construct a new choice of law rule limited to new categories of rules (such as trusts or quasi-contracts), and a result selecting principle is advanced. This doctrine is therefore less ambitious than that of Currie.[265] Moreover, it retains the notion of choice of law rules. Like the doctrine of governmental interests, it looks to the rules of substantive law, and only to the rules of substantive law, of a restricted number of legal systems.[266] It considers only the personal law, which is that of the home State and territorial law, which is the law in which a certain activity or result has manifested itself.[267] Thus the question arises, once again, whether the initial selection of potentially applicable laws is made on the strength of overriding principles, namely those of the American Constitution, or in virtue of the unfettered discretion of the *lex fori*. Once again it would seem that an overriding principle forms the basic assumption, and once again the reliance on the notion of false conflicts supports this conclusion.[268] In a conflict between these rival laws, all of which can claim attention (so it would seem) by virtue of the overriding principle, that rule is to be applied which, after weighing the purposes of the various rules for selection [269] deserves to be preferred. Such preferences, expressed in abstract propositions, are expected to supply a sufficient number of principles of preference combining spatial and substantive criteria within a framework of creative justice which accommodates conflicting laws [270] and provides predictability.[271]

Seven such principles are put forward by way of example. Shorn of their special terminology and expressed in terms of orthodox rules of conflict of laws, they proclaim—

(1) In a conflict between the *lex personalis (lex larium et penatium)* of the defendant, the *lex loci actus* and the *lex loci injuriae*, the

lex loci injuriae applies if it requires a higher standard of conduct or accords higher financial protection than the other two laws.[272]

Exception: if the injured person and the person causing the injury stand in a special relationship towards each other, the law governing their relationship applies.

(2) In a conflict between the *lex personalis* of the plaintiff (see above (1)), the *lex loci actus* and the *lex loci injuriae*, the laws of the *lex loci actus* and the *lex loci injuriae*, if the same, apply, if they set a lower standard of conduct or of financial protection than the *lex personalis.*[273]

Exception: the same exception as in Principle (1).

Proviso *(a)*: If the *leges personales* of the injured party and the tortfeasor are both more exacting than the *lex loci delicti,* the less exacting of the former applies.[274]

Proviso *(b)*: In a conflict between the *lex personalis* of the injured party and the *lex loci delicti,* concerning claims for wrongful death and survival of actions in tort, the *lex personalis* applies.[275]

(3) In a conflict between the *lex loci actus* and the *lex loci injuriae,* the *lex loci actus* applies if it has "established special controls, including the sanction of civil liability", even if the standards of conduct and financial protection of the *lex loci injuriae* are less exacting.[276]

Proviso: if the *lex loci actus* enacts a law with the dual purpose of regulating an activity and of safeguarding property, the latter purpose, if predominant, excludes the application of the *lex loci actus* in favour of the *lex loci injuriae* which is less exacting.[277]

(4) In a conflict between the law of the State in which a relationship has its seat and the *lex loci delicti,* the law governing the relationship applies if it has imposed on one party to the relationship a standard of conduct or of financial protection for the benefit of the other party which is higher than that imposed by the *lex loci delicti.*[278]

Proviso: In a conflict between the personal laws of the parties and the *lex loci delicti* on the one hand and the law of the State in which a relationship between the parties has its seat, on the other hand, the former, if less exacting, applies.[279]

(5) In a conflict between the law of the State in which a relationship has its seat and the *lex loci injuriae*, the law governing the relationship

applies if it has imposed on one party to the relationship a standard of conduct or of financial protection for the benefit of the other party which is lower than that imposed by the *lex loci injuriae*.[280]

(6) In a conflict between the *lex personalis*, which protects a person from his own incompetence, heedlessness, ignorance and unequal bargaining power by restricting that person's power to contract or to convey or encumber property, and any other law, the personal law applies, if the transaction or property concerned is centred in the State which provides the personal law or if it is not so centred by chance or due to *fraude à la loi*.[281]

Proviso 1: If the protective law envisages certain types of transactions and not classes of persons, the law of the place applies where the transaction is centred,[282] presumably if the latter law does not coincide with the *lex personalis*.

Proviso 2: If the personal law of the promisor provides protection and the law of the place where the transaction is centred denies protection, the law which denies special protection to the promisor and upholds the agreement may have to be applied.[283]

(7) Free choice of law is admitted if the law so chosen is reasonably related to the transaction, and permits the performance of it, although neither party has his home in the State, the law of which is chosen, and although the transaction is not centred there, provided that no protective law applicable under Principle No. (6) is in issue or that the transaction concerns land and is contrary to mandatory rules of the *lex situs*. The legal effect of the transaction on third parties with independent interests is not determined by this principle.[284]

Section 19. The International Use of the New Doctrines

36. The modern American doctrines promulgated by Currie, Cavers and a number of other writers [285] with some variations can now be examined in their setting.

Both doctrines look to substantive law in order to make a choice; Currie relies on the expression of governmental interests and applies the *lex fori* if it has an interest and even if it has none, provided that several foreign laws have an interest to apply. The application of foreign law is thus restricted or possibly excluded, leaving the dispute to be decided in a more convenient forum. Cavers looks to the purpose of the various of law and selects that rule which produces the better result.[286] Both doctrines look to a number of laws or rules which are drawn from a variety of legal systems, which is, however, limited. The limitation is determined by a number of tests (known as connecting factors, to be discussed below) calling on the consideration of the laws of States which are concerned either because the transaction or event is connected with their territory or because the parties involved have their home in one or the other of these States. The need to consider all these laws appears to be dictated by an overriding principle of the American Constitution requiring equal respect for the laws of all Member States together with that of the forum.

37. Faced with a choice imposed by an overriding principle, Currie examines the governmental interests shown by the rules of the States concerned and resolves the problem either by relying on the *lex fori* or the *lex gravitatis unicae*; Cavers embarks upon a cumulation of the rules embodied in the various legal systems which are potentially applicable, and seeks one in accordance with a preference expressed by the *forum* in the terms of a choice of law rule. The difference between orthodox choice of law rules (to be analysed, *infra*, Part III) and those advocated here is that the former are expressed in terms of formal categories of rules which are connected with particular countries by a series of formal connecting factors; the latter are in addition, expressed in terms of substantive categories of rules advantageous or disadvantageous to the plaintiff. Both doctrines thus seek to pinpoint a rule forming part of a particular system of laws out of a number available for consideration. The need to consider foreign legal systems, otherwise than by an act of initial discretion (as European systems of Private International Law do), and the aim to apply objective criteria of choice which are not arbitrary and accord full respect to the rules in a number of legal systems is explained by the practice of the Supreme Court of the United States of America. The court, as will be remembered, requires the rules of the conflict of laws of the Member States to be so constructed that they give weight to the various governmental interests involved while administering justice between the parties. Both doctrines which were examined above seek to satisfy these requirements; Currie attaches preponderant importance to governmental interests, while Cavers is moved by the need to do justice in the individual case without jettisoning principle and certainty.

38. The conclusion must be, therefore, that the doctrines reflect the need in the federal system of the United States to adapt general, unfettered choice of law rules, as they are known in the Private International Law dealing with conflicts of laws between different States, to the demands of the Constitution. The conclusion suggested here, namely that these doctrines were conceived in order to satisfy the particular needs of the conflict of laws under the American Constitution, is borne out by another consideration. Both make much play with so-called "false conflicts" which must be disregarded. In fact they are disregarded in Europe and elsewhere, because no party will raise an issue of conflict of laws if the rules in both systems of law are identical in form or in their effect or do not purport to apply. On the other hand, the failure to consider the law of a sister State which is the same or has the same effect as that applied by the forum may stimulate a constitutional complaint. The fact that in the opinion of the court only one country has an interest in the case may be a good reason for denying constitutional review if a rule taken from that legal system is applied, but outside the United States the existence or not of an established rule of Private International Law counts first, except *de lege ferenda*.

39. The two doctrines may be suited to the needs of the United States where orthodox rules of the conflict of laws form part of the domestic law of the Member States, must operate concurrently with other rules of the conflict of laws in sister States and are subject to the overriding control of the Constitution. The homogeneous character of American private law, which is based on the common law, except in Louisiana, may assist in fostering their success, and the relatively small number of situations involving the application of foreign law (mainly in the field of contract and tort) may help. In these areas the need is clear for the development of new, detailed and sophisticated rules of conflict of laws. The problem remains whether the standards of control developed by the Supreme Court of the United States can serve themselves as rules of the conflict of laws or at least as the basis for such rules in the law of the Member States and in the federal courts or whether the principles elaborated by the Supreme Court are and remain general standards to which individual systems of conflict of laws must conform, while retaining their individual identity. Apparently, the Supreme Court itself has expressed the belief at least on one occasion [287] that a new system of conflict of laws is emerging; many modern writers seem to think so, but it will be for the practice and, if need be, the legislature to formulate

such rules. As shown above, the task is not an easy one.

Confronted with a conflict of laws involving a tort and a guest statute, the New York Court of Appeals has recently paid less attention to the existence of governmental interests as expressed in implied spatial or personal considerations attached to rules of substantive law or to considerations of the better law. Instead it has resorted to the technique of ascertaining the law most closely connected with the issue by cumulating the usual connecting factors most intimately concerned in an order of successive combinations operating alternatively which proceed from the closest personal to the more distant objective contacts.[287a] This approach corresponds to that adopted by the Hague Convention on the Law applicable to Traffic Accidents of 2 October 1973.

It is quite another problem whether countries outside the federal system of the United States should heed the voices from the United States. This will depend in part on the result of the discussion whether Private International Law outside a federal system is subject to overriding principles of Public International Law.[288] In part it has been answered above [289] when it was pointed out that the differing character of legal systems outside the United States makes it possible, at best to ascertain their function [290] and to characterise them, but makes it impracticable to determine the real interests and ulterior purposes of rules of foreign law.

Section 20. Conclusions

40. Private International Law, like any other branch of domestic law, is determined partly by tradition and partly by policy. Since it is of recent growth, the importance of policy in its development is greater than in other branches of law which can look back to a longer history. For the same reason it has relied more upon doctrine than is usual in domestic law. Only Public International Law has drawn on writers to an even greater extent. Although these factors make for diversity rather than uniformity the following trends emerge:

First, there is a tendency to hold that all rules of domestic law contain their own limitations in space. These limitations are said to arise from the nature of these rules, from the fact that they concern persons or property, from their social purpose or governmental interest or from the expression of characteristics peculiar to the nation to which a person belongs. By their nature these doctrines are universalistic.

Second, there is a tendency to hold that all rules of law, whether local or foreign, are applied in accordance with the territorial division of legal systems and in deference to the sovereign character of States. Some believe that this division determines with universal effect when local and when foreign law applies. Others, taking a more one-sided view, believe that the territorial division of legal systems can only determine whether local law applies and where its sphere of application ends.[291] Others again, relying more upon the tie of sovereignty than upon the territorial division of States as a link between the law of a country, its territory and its subjects, assert that it is thus possible to determine the sphere of local law to situations at home and abroad. Still others, by way of generalising the last assumption, state that the division of sovereignties determines not only whether local law applies to situations which arise abroad but also whether foreign law applies to situations which arise locally. All these doctrines rely upon the division of sovereignty or the territoriality of law. They are all international no matter whether they purport to lay down with universal validity general principles of Private International Law or unilateral rules determining when local law and when foreign law must be applied, or whether they claim to be particularist by determining exclusively when local law must be applied to situations abroad without touching upon the question when foreign law must be applied to situations which arise locally or abroad.

While it is not possible to accept these doctrines as a general basis of Private International Law, it must be admitted that they are of limited validity.

In the first place modern systems of Private International Law were first developed within States which possessed composite systems of law.[292] The existence of a central authority with overriding powers to delimit the sphere of operation of individual legislation and the application of law by the courts in the member States encourages the doctrine of territoriality of laws. Modern American doctrines reflect this historical inheritance coupled with an unconscious return to an even older way of thinking.

In the second place, there are certain branches of law, primarily of a public law nature,[293] where the problem is one of establishing the respective frontiers of legislation, but never that of applying foreign substantive law. In general, rules of Private International Law can be unilateral or bilateral, but when concerned with the application of private law they must always deal with the two-fold problem of when the *lex fori* and when foreign law must be applied. Certain branches of Conflict of Laws, however, rely exclusively upon unilateral rules, for the reason that they are concerned with a process of self-limitation and not with a process of choice of law. The law of procedure is such a branch, and the law of bankruptcy is another, as are the law of taxation, administrative law and modern anti-trust and currency legislation. The forum never applies such foreign laws. It is only concerned with the limits of operation of local and foreign laws bearing the character of public law, but the latter can be taken into account as a fact or datum.[294] The principle of territoriality based upon the division of legislative spheres fulfils its proper function here.

Third, there is a trend from the time of Wächter onwards to regard Private International Law as part of domestic law, determined by considerations of domestic policy, circumscribed by domestic legislation and unfettered by limitations arising from the person, area or nature and purpose of a rule of law as such. Its task is to introduce categories of rules of foreign law, or individual rules of foreign law to be applied to types of situations or to particular situations or events. The only legal controls are exercised by Public International Law among the community of States and by constitutional law among the Member States of a specific Federal State. The restrictions on an unbridled choice of law which can be imposed by constitutional law in a Federal State were discussed above when the influence of the Constitution upon and the practice of the Supreme Court of the United States were examined as they affect rules of the conflict of laws in the United States.[295] It remains, therefore, to turn last to the relationship between Public International Law and Private International Law.

NOTES TO PART I

1. Savigny, *Geschichte des Römischen Rechts im Mittelalter*, VI (2 ed.) 229; Gutzwiller in *Festschrift für Tuor* (1946), pp. 145, 167, n. 55; Meijers, *Hague Rec.* 49 (1934 III), 543, at p. 614.
2. Prosser, (1953) 51 *Mich. L. Rev.* 959, 971; De Nova, *Hague Rec.* 118 (1966 II), 434.
3. See the bibliography in Ehrenzweig, *Hague Rec.* 124 (1968 II), 169, at p. 179, n. 2; to these should now be added:

(2) *Latin-America:* Vieira, 130 (1970 II), 351; *Yugoslavia:* Katičić 131 (1970 III), 393; *USA:* Cavers, 131 (1970 III), 75; Willis Reese, 133 (1971 II), 421.

(3) Valladão, 133 (1971 II), 421; Loussouarn, 139 (1973 II), 275; Kahn-Freund, 143 (1974 III), 139; Lalive, 155 (1977 II), 1; Philip, 160 (1978) II), 1.
(4) *Reciprocity:* Lagarde, 154 (1971 I), 103; *Personal Status:* Salah el Dine Tarazi, 159 (1978 I), 345; *Particularism:* Carillo Salcedo, 160 (1978 II), 181.
(5) *Constitutional Aspects:* Castel, 126 (1969 I), 1; *Rivers:* Koutikov, 127 (1969 II), 247; *Contracts between State and Individual:* Weil, 128 (1969 III), 94; *Nationality and Domicile:* de Winter, 128 (1969 III), 346; *Maritime Law:* Rodière, 135 (1972 I), 329; (flag): Bonassis, 128 (1969 III), 504; *Restrictive Practices:* Goldman, 128 (1969 III), 631; *Agency:* Schmitthoff, 130 (1970 I), 109; *Relation to Public Law:* Mann, 132 (1971 I), 109; *Bankruptcy:* Pastor Ridruejo, 133 (1971 II), 135; *Jurisdiction:* Miaja de la Muela, 135 (1972 I), 1; *Transactions between States, Foreign Public and Private Firms:* Goldschmidt, 136 (1972 II), 203; *Obligations in the Foreign Commerce of Socialist States:* Skapski, 136 (1972 II), 499; *Party Autonomy:* Curti-Gialdino, 137 (1972 III), 743; *Inter-Personal Law:* Szászy, 138 (1973 I), 81; *Torts in Socialist Countries:* Czachorski, 139 (1973 II), 387; *Succession:* Murad Ferid, 142 (1974 II), 71; *Contracts:* Vischer, 142 (1974 II), 1; *Matrimonial Property:* Droz, 143 (1974 III), 1; *Prorogatio and Derogatio Fori:* Jodlowski, 143 (1974 III), 475; *Commercial Arbitration:* Sanders, 145 (1975 II), 205; *Relation between Contract and Tort:* Ferrari-Bravo, 145 (1975 III), 341; *Multinational Companies:* Kopelmanas, 145 (1976 II), 295; *Monetary Laws:* Malaurie, 160 (1978 II), 265.
(8) *Conventions:* Vitta, 126 (1969 I), 110 von Overbeck, 132 (1971 I), 1; *Between Socialist Countries:* Sósniak, 144 (1975 I), 1.
(9) *Peremptory Norms:* Eek, 139 (1973 II), 1; *Pluralism of Methods:* Batiffol, 139 (1973 II), 75; *Private International Law in the Non-Unified Legal Systems:* Graveson, 141 (1974 I), 187; *Codification:* Ferrer-Correia, 145 (1975 II), 57.

4. See below sec. 20, pp. 44-46; sec. 25, pp. 80-81.

5. See below sec. 21, pp. 63-67.

6. But see now the Third French Draft of a law on P.I.L. amending the Civil Code. Foyer, *Clunet* 1971, 31; Reichelt, *Z.f.Rv.*, 12 (1971), 249; Nadelmann and von Mehren, (1970), 18 *AJCL*, 614.

7. See below sec. 10, pp. 17-19.

8. Huber, *Praelectiones Juris Romani et Hodierni* II, 1, 3, 2; Rodenburg, *de Statutorum Diversitate* I, 3, 4, cited by Story, *Commentaries*, para. 25.

9. Evrigenis, *Hague Rec.* 118 (1966 II), 319, at p. 320, n. 2 with lit.

10. See below sec. 25, pp. 80-81.

11. See below sec. 21, pp. 63-67.

12. Evrigenis, *loc. cit.*, p. 322 with lit.

13. Lewald in *Archeion tou Idiotikou Dikaiou*, 13 (1946), 30-78; *Labeo*, 5 (1959), 335-369; *Rev. critique de droit international privé*, 1968, 419-440, 615-639; Taubenschlag, *The Law of Graeco-Roman Egypt in the light of the Papyri* (1944), *Opera Minora*, I, II (1959), *passim*; Maridakis, *Melanges Streit*, I (1939), 575; Bickermann, *Arch. f. Pap. Forschung* VIII (1927), 225; Wenger, *Studi Bonfante* II (1930), 465, 473 n. 7; Mommsen, *Ges. Schriften* II (1905) 144; Wlassak, *Römische Prozessgesetze* II (1891), 126; Schönbauer, *ZSS* 49 (1929), 345; *Anz. Oest. AK Wiss, Phil.-Hist. Klasse* 97 (1960), 182.

14. Savigny, VIII, pp. 78 ff.; Baviera, "Diritto internazionale di Roma", *Arch. giur.*, 61 (1898), 243; for texts see Wächter, *Archiv f. d. civ. Praxis*, 24 (1841), 230 at pp. 242 ff.; Meili in *Zeitschrift für internationales Privatrecht*, 9 (1899), pp. 3 ff.; Gutzwiller, *Hague Rec.*, p. 308, n. 1, and in *Festschrift für Tuor* (1946), 145 at p. 162, n. 32. And see David in *Symbolae van Oven* (1946), pp. 231-250; Niederer in *Festschrift für Fritzsche* (1952), pp. 115-132; *Rev. critique de droit international privé*, 1960, pp. 137-150; F. de Vischer, *Antiquité classique*, 13 (1945), 11;

ibid., 14 (1946), 29; *Rev. de la Soc. Jean Bodin*, 9 (1958), 195; Volterra, *Travaux et Conférences de la Faculté de droit de l'Université libre de Bruxelles*, III (1955), 135-155; *Annuario di diritto internazionale*, 1 (1965), 553-562, and see the literature cited by de Nova, p. 443, n. 1. And see also Sturm, *Clunet* 1979, 259 with further literature.

15. Savigny, *Geschichte*, I (1815), p. 90 ff.; Neumeyer, *Die gemeinrechtliche Entwicklung des internationalen Privat- und Strafrechts bis Bartolus*, I (1901), *passim*; Hamaker, *Rechtsgeleerd Magazijn*, 22 (1903), p. 133; Stutz, *Zeitschrift der Savigny Stiftung* (Germ.Abt.), 26 (1905), p. 354; Beckmann, *Zeitschrift für vergleichende Rechtswissenschaft*, 1 (1907), pp. 394 ff.; Ernst Mayer, *Zeitschrift der Savigny Stiftung* (Germ.Abt.), 38 (1917), pp. 373 ff.; Meijers, *Bejdrage tot de geschiedenis van het International Privaat- en Strafrecht in Frankrijk en de Nederlanden* (1914) = *Etudes d'histoire du droit international privé* (1967); *Hague Rec.* 49 (1934 III), 543, 548 ff.; same in *Tijdschrift voor Rechtsgeschiedenis*, 3 (1922), pp. 61 ff.; van Hove, *ibid.*, 3 (1922), p. 277; Stobbe, *Jahrbücher des gemeinen Rechts*, 6 (1863), pp. 21 ff.; Niederer, *Einführung* (2 ed. 1956), pp. 23-31, and see the literature cited by de Nova, *Hague Rec.* 118 (1966 II), at p. 443, n. 1.

16. Subject to emerging local customs; Neumeyer, I, 40, but generally the dichotomy is clear: Neumeyer, I, 50, 80 ff., 121.

17. Agubardi ep. ad Lud. P.; see Boucquet, *Rerum Gallicarum et Franciarum Scriptores* (1738), Vol. 6, p. 356; Savigny, *Geschichte* (2 ed. 1834), Vol. I, p. 116; Neumeyer, I, 10, see also 62, 85-87, 144; Meijers, *Hague Rec.* at p. 561-562; *Mon. Germ., Epistolae* V, 159; Migne, 104 col. 116.

18. E.g., nobody loses a right, except under his own law; claims arising out of a crime attract the law of the injured person.

19. Neumeyer, I, 89, 111-112 ff., 119, 155.

20. Neumeyer, I, 94, 98, 107, 155, 158.

21. Neumeyer, I, 123, 136, 160, 168.

22. Neumeyer, I, 58, 65, 92, 127, 141, 145, 156, 160.

23. Neumeyer, I, 144, 146 (as a result of the disappearance of tribal divisions and loyalties), 160, 162, 165, esp. 166.

24. Neumeyer, I, 106: first for criminal law, procedure, majority, 145, 169, 170 (continued co-existence of local and tribal law), 171.

25. Neumeyer, I, 170.

26. Neumeyer, I, 172.

27. Neumeyer, I, 175; cp. I, p. 231.

28. Neumeyer, I, 175.

29. Meijers, *Hague Rec.* 49 (1934 III), p. 543, at pp. 567 ff.; Gutzwiller, *Hague Rec.* 29 (1929 IV), 29; see also Wächter, *A.c.P.*, 24 (1841), pp. 280 ff.; 25 (1842), pp. 1 ff.; pp. 361 ff.; Lainé, *Introduction au droit international privé*, I (1888), 1-296; Neumeyer, II (1916); same in *Zeitschrift für vergleichende Rechtswissenschaft*, 11 (1917), 190 ff.; Yntema (1953), 2 *A.J.Comp.Law*, 297-317; De Nova, *Hague Rec.* 118 (1966 II); for the canonist literature see Oudin, *Revue de droit international et de droit comparé*, 31 (1953), pp. 16-25.

30. The proper court is that of the place where the interested party in personal matters or in matters of succession had his home. Meijers, *loc. cit.*, pp. 573, 575.

31. Meijers, *Hague Rec.*, at p. 583. For movables the jurisdiction was vested in the court before which the original transfer had been made; see Wächter, *A.c.P.*, 24 (1841), p. 230, at p. 254, n. 1; Sachsenspiegel, III.33.1.30; Schwabenspiegel c. 286. No clear cut rules were developed for torts. Procedure was always governed by the *lex fori*, but evidence remained linked to the personal law of the parties.

32. Ehrenzweig.

33. For the treaty practice of the Italian City States, which laid the foundations of their domestic practices, see Neumeyer, II, pp. 9-56; Meijers, *Hague Rec.*, at pp. 592 ff.

34. Meijers, *Hague Rec.* 49 (1934 III), p. 594, n. 1; the attribution to Carolus de Tocco, rather than to Roffredus, Neumeyer, II, 75, was made by Meijers in *Atti del Congresso internazionale di diritto romano*, I (1934), 431, at p. 469.

35. For texts setting out his opinion see Neumeyer, II, 58, n. 3; Balduinus seems to have shared this opinion, at least initially; Neumeyer, II, 63, 76.

36. Neumeyer, II, 61-63, 76 n. 1, for the authorship of the text which is regarded by Neumeyer as an addition after 1228 to the Accursian gloss; "Pone: duo litigant coram judice in casu determinato; una est consuetudo in loco rei, alia est consutudo in loco actoris, alia in loco judicis. Per quam consuetuetudinem terminabitur." See also Gutzwiller, p. 303; Bellapertica C 1.1.1. ad. legem cunctos populos, No. 14; Meijers, *Bijdrage*, Annex 5, xxxi; *Etudes de droit international privé*, p. 130.

37. See the text and comment given by Meijers, *Hague Rec.*, p. 595.

38. Neumeyer, II, pp. 66-68; see also the treaties (1181, 1191, 1237) cited p. 69, note; Tilsch, *Rev. dr. int. et de legisl. comparée* (2nd ser.), 13 (1911), p. 417; Gutzwiller, p. 301, n. 1.

39. Neumeyer, II, pp. 70-71.

40. Gutzwiller, p. 302.

41. Neumeyer, II, pp. 80, 83, n. 1, 71, 84.

42. Neumeyer, II, 89.

43. Neumeyer, II, 85-87; Lainé, I, 253, see also 121, 135, 177, 189, 204; Gutzwiller, *Hague Rec.* 29 (1929 IV), p. 304; Meijers, *ibid.*, 49 (1939 IV), 597.

44. Except for contracts concluded abroad (see Revigny cited above, p. 7, n. 46; for the application of foreign law during this period see the proposal of Aldricus, above p. 111; Neumeyer, II, p. 101. The conclusions are only negative in the sense that they restrict the operation of the *lex fori*; see Neumeyer, II, p. 99.

45. See Meijers, *Hague Rec.*, p. 597 ff.

46. Revigny (Ravanis) was a pupil of Jac. Balduinus—Lainé, I, 120; for Revigny see ad D.5.1.1 (1. si subiiciant), Meijers, *Nieuwe Bijdrage*, p. 82; *Etudes d'histoire du droit*, III, p. 139 (6); the *lex loci contractus, lex delicti, lex rei sitae,* all served as choice of law rules; see also p. 140 (8) ad D.13.4.2.1 (1. arbitraria actio); (9) ad C.7.33.12 (1. Quicum in longi temporis prescriptione), *Bijdrage*, Annex XX; *Etudes d'histoire du droit*, III, p. 140; *Etudes d'histoire du droit international privé*, p. 127 (4).

47. See above n. 46.

48. Ad legem Cunctos populos 1.1.1.1: Dominus meus dicit: semper est inspicienda loci consuetudo in quo res sunt (arg. legum allegatarum, D.26.7.42.2; D.26.5.27); Meijers, *Hague Rec.*, at p. 597; *Etudes d'histoire du droit international privé* (1967), p. 126 (1) end; *Etudes d'histoire du droit*, III (1959), 133, 135 (1) end; Meijers, *Nieuwe Bijdrage*, p. 86; *Etudes d'histoire du droit*, III, 146; and see Meijers, *Hague Rec.*, at p. 599: "pour Pierre de Belleperche, une coutume personnelle n'est rien qu'une coutume qui, à l'instar d'une action personnelle, prescrit de donner ou faire quelque chose. La coutume réelle donne, à l'instar de l'action réelle, une déclaration des droits réels de personnes intéressées."

49. Lainé, I, 121-122; Meijers, *Hague Rec.*, p. 598. For Bellapertica's views on this distinction see ad Inst., 1, 2, n. 45-46.

50. See, e.g., Bellapertica ad 1. Cunctos populos, Meijers, *Nieuwe Bijdrage*, p. 88; *Etudes d'histoire du droit*, III, pp. 141, 142 (8); *Etudes d'histoire du dr.i.p.* p. 129, App. V, at p. 133.

51. Neumeyer, II, pp. 78, 80.

52. See above, p. 7, n. 44.

53. Meijers, *Hague Rec.*, p. 599 and n. 2.

54. Meijers, *Hague Rec.*, p. 600.

55. Ullmann (1949) 64 *English Historical Review*, 1 ff.; *History of Political Thought* (1965), p. 197; Gutzwiller, *Hague Rec.*, at p. 314, n. 3 and the writers cited there. The interpretation given by Mann, *Hague Rec.* 111 (1964 I), at pp. 24-25, is influenced by notions developed in later centuries.

56. 1303; a thesis pronounced by the lawyers of Philippe le Bel; see Chénon, *Histoire générale du droit français public et privé*, I (1926), pp. 526, 817; Gutzwiller, *Hague Rec.*, at pp. 306 ff.; Neumeyer, II. ch. 3.

For the canonist view see Régout, *La doctrine de la guerre juste* (1935), pp. 54, 82 (Thomist theory), 87, 100, esp. 125 (Cajetanus), 145; Ives de la Brière, *Le droit de juste guerre* (1938), pp. 59-60, citing Alanus: *"Unus quisque enim (illorum) tantum juris habit in regno suo quantum imperator in imperio"*; see also J. Rivière, *Le problème de l'Eglise et de l'Etat au temps de Philippe de Bel* (1926), p. 428; van Hove, *Tijdschrift voor Rechtsgeschiedenis*, III (1922), p. 277; Gutzwiller, *Festschrift für Tuor* (1946), at p. 163, n. 4; Oudin, *Rev. de droit international et de droit comparé*, 31 (1954), Suppl., pp. 16-25; Belgian Reports to the 4th Congress of the International Academy of Comparative Law. But see Meijers, *Hague Rec.*, at p. 630 and n. 1.

57. For lit. see Gutzwiller, *Hague Rec.*, 316, n. 3, especially as regards editions of texts: Meili, *Die theoretischen Abhandlungen des Bartolus und Baldus über das internationale Privat- und Strafrecht, Niemeyer's Z.*, 4 (1894), pp. 258, 340, 446; Guthrie's transl. of Savigny, *System des heutigen römischen Rechts*, Vol. 8 (2 ed. Edinburgh, 1880), App. I; Beale, *Bartolus on the Conflict of Laws* (Cambridge, Mass. 1914); Smith (1970), 14 *Am. J. Legal History* 157, 247; but see the critique of Ehrenzweig (1963), 12 *A.J.Comp.L.*, 384; Meili in *Festschrift für Laband* (1908); Lainé, I, 131; Surville in *Clunet* 1921, p. 5.

58. For lit. see Meijers, *Hague Rec.*, at p. 606; Gutzwiller, *Hague Rec.*, p. 320, n. 2, and in *Festschrift für Tuor* (1946), pp. 145-178; Meili, *loc. cit.*, above n. 57; Lainé, I, 166; Bonolis, *Questioni di diritto internazionale in alcuni consigli inediti di Baldo* (1908).

59. Gutzwiller, *loc. cit.*, p. 305. Meijers, *Hague Rec.*, pp. 600 ff.

60. Meijers, *Bijdrage*, Annex XVI; *Hague Rec.*, pp. 602, 603, 605; *Etudes d'histoire de droit*, III (1959), 283, 286 n. 7; *Tijdschrift voor Rechtsgeschiedenis*, 16 (1939), 114, 117, n. 3.

61. Statutum reale: quod disponit circa rem; statutum personale: quod disponit circa personam.

62. Lainé, I, 137.

63. Lainé, I, 138.

64. Bartolus, *Commentarii in Codicem* (C.1.11.), Nos. 32, 39, 40, 41; Cp. Lainé, I, 132, 146, 150.

65. Cp. Lainé, I, 153 ff., 171 ff.

66. Bartolus, *loc. cit.*, No. 33; Lainé, I, 157; Meijers, *Hague Rec.*, at pp. 601, 608, 630 ff.

67. Baldus C.1.1.1.1., No. 91; Angelus cons. 210; Meijers, p. 531. Many doubts existed: was the rule which postponed females to males in intestate succession, or the prohibition of gifts between spouses, whether *inter vivos* or by will, *odiosa* or *favorabilis*, seeing that the disability imposed upon one party is always balanced by a benefit conferred upon another? See Meijers, *Hague Rec.*, pp. 618-610, 630; Bartolus, *loc. cit.*, No. 33.

68. Meijers, *Hague Rec.*, at p. 607.

69. Revigny, Belleperche, ad 1. Cunctos populos; Meijers, *Bijdrage*, Annex XXI;

Etudes d'histoire du droit, III, 141, 144; *Etudes d'histoire du d.i.p.*, p. 129, at 132.

70. Guillaume de Cun, ad 1. Cunctos populos, Meijers, *Etudes d'histoire du d.i.p.*, p. 135, at 136, 137.

71. "Verba consuetudinis attendenda sunt"; see Meijers, *Bijdrage*, Annex XXVIII; *Etudes d'histoire du droit international privé*, Appendix VI, p. 135, at p. 137.

72. Bartolus, *loc. cit.*, No. 42; Meijers, *Hague Rec.*, at p. 608.

73. Bartolus, *loc. cit.*, No. 43. The French school regarded the law of the domicile of choice as the *lex personalis*; the Italian school relied on the law of the domicile of origin.

74. Bartolus, *loc. cit.*, No. 43; Lainé, I, 156; see a similar solution given by Guillaume de Cun, above, p. 10, n. 71.

75. For the treatment of this question by Bartolus see Gutzwiller, *Hague Rec.*, p. 319; Lainé, I, 154 ff., 158. For the lit. on the "English question" see Gutzwiller, *Hague Rec.*, at pp. 315, n. 1, 319; in *Festschrift für Tuor* (1946), p. 145, at 164; Meijers, *Bijdrage*, Annex XVIII and text, p. 92; Bellapertica ad 1. Cunctos populos cited above, p. 10, n. 69. D'Argentré's comment was: *Nihil potest dici futilius*, cited by Wächter, *A.c.P.*, 24 (1841), p. 230, at p. 274, n. 79; Hertius: *Verum in iis definiendis mirum est quam sudent Doctores*; Wächter, *loc. cit.*, p. 278, n. 90, and generally pp. 278 ff. Another example is: *conjux conjugi ne donato*; Wächter, *loc. cit.*, at p. 257; Meijers, *Hague Rec.*, p. 617 and n. 4; Lainé, I, 160-161.

76. For cases see Meijers, *Hague Rec.*, at pp. 617 ff.

77. Meijers, *Hague Rec.*, at pp. 308-309, and n. 1.

78. Meijers, *loc. cit.*, p. 609.

79. See also Meijers, *Hague Rec.*, at p. 629.

80. See below, sec. 9, pp. 13-16.

81. See Gutzwiller, *Hague Rec.*, at p. 312.

82. See Meijers, *Hague Rec.*, p. 630.

83. Meijers, *ibid.*, p. 633 ff.

84. Gutzwiller, *Hague Rec.* 29 (1929 IV), p. 230; Meylan in *Mélanges Fournier* (1929), p. 511; Meili in *Niemeyer's Z.*, 5 (1895), pp. 362, 452; Lainé, I, 223; Laborderie, *Clunet* 1921, p. 79; Gamillscheg, *Der Einfluss Dumoulin's auf die Entwicklung des Kollisionsrechts* (1955).

85. Gutzwiller, *loc. cit.*; Meili, *loc. cit.*, at p. 371; Lainé, I, 311; Barbey, *Rev. hist. de droit français et étranger*, 19-20 (1940-41), 397 ff.; de Nova, *Hague Rec.* 118 (1966 II), at pp. 447-448.

86. For details see especially Meijers, *loc. cit.*, at pp. 639, 640, n. 3, 641; Wächter, *A.c.P.*, 24 (1841), at p. 295, n. 132; p. 302, n. 147; 25 (1842), p. 190, n. 136, p. 384.

87. For details see Meijers, *loc. cit.*, pp. 645, 649, 652, who attributes (p. 610) the earliest reliance on the intention of a party to Butrigarius.

88. For details see Meijers, *Hague Rec.* 49 (1934 IV), pp. 637, 641.

89. For lit. see Gutzwiller, *Hague Rec.* 29 (1929 IV), p. 325, n. 2; see also Meijers, *Hague Rec.* 49 (1934 III), at pp. 663-670; de Nova, *Hague Rec.* 118 (1966 II), at pp. 448-451 and the writers cited below in n. 92 and at p. 14, n. 97.

90. See above, p. 6.

91. Gutzwiller, *Hague Rec.*, at p. 326.

92. See Yntema, in *Vom deutschen zum europäischen Recht*, II (1963), p. 65 at p. 74; (1966), 65 *Mich.L.R.*, 1 at p. 18; (1963), 12 *A.J.Comp.L.*, 474.

93. See Huber, *Praelectiones Juris Civilis Romani et hodierni* (1689), II. 1. 3. 12.

94. *De statutis eorumque concursu* (1661), 4. 2. 17; Gutzwiller, *loc. cit.*, p. 326, n. 1; Meijers, *Hague Rec.*, p. 664, n. 1 with further texts; Yntema, *loc. cit.*, p. 78, n. 37; Grotius, *De jure belli ac pacis* lib. 1, cap. III, para. 21.2.

95. *Mobilium et immobilium natura* (1666); Gutzwiller, *loc. cit.*, p. 326, n. 1.

96. Gutzwiller, p. 327, n. 1. See Yntema, *loc. cit.*, 79.

97. *Praelectiones*, II. 1.3.2; *Heedendaegse Rechtsgeleerthejt*, I. 3.4; *De jure civitatis*, III. 4.1.14. For the text of the *Praelectiones* see Lorenzen (1919), 13 *Ill.L.R.*, 375; *Selected Articles* (1947), pp. 136 ff.; Llewelfryn Davies (1937), 18 *British Yb.Int.L.*, 49; Meili, *Zeitschrift für Internationales Privatrecht*, 7 (1898), p. 189; see also 3 *Dallas* 370-377 (1797)—see Nadelmann in *Jus et Lex, Festgabe für Gutzwiller* (1959), 263 at p. 267; Lainé, II, 199; Gutzwiller, *loc. cit.*, p. 327, n. 1. For variants in the text of *De jure civitatis* see Kollewijn, *Geschiedenis van de Nederlandse Wetenschap van het Internationaal Privaatrecht tot 1880* (1937), p. 132.

98. *Praelectiones*, II, 1. 3.2; *Heedendaegse Rechtsgeleerthejt*, I.3.5; *De jure civitatis, loc. cit.*; "intra terminos eius exercita" (Rodenburg). See Yntema, *loc. cit.*, p. 76.

99. *Praelectiones*, II, 1.3.2; *Heedendaegse Rechtsgeleerthejt*, I. 3, 6; *De jure civitatis*, III. 4.1 (3 ed.); III, 10 (1st ed.). The Dutch text (*Heedendaegse Rechtsgeleerthejt*) is significant: it says: "de hooge machten van yder landt bieden elkander de handt ten einde de rechten van yder op elk syn onderdanen, schoon elders zynde soo verre gelden, als het niet is strydig met de macht of het recht van des anderen in syn bedryf"; cp. Asser, *Schets van het International Privaatrecht*, Intr.s.5: international benevolence, Evrigenis, *loc. cit.*, p. 326.

100. Meijers, *Hague Rec.*, at p. 664, demonstrates the difference between the terms "de summo jure", "de necessitate" on the one hand, and of "de humanitate", "de comitate" on the other hand. See also Yntema, *op. cit.*, II, p. 76, n. 30; p. 79, n. 40, n. 44.

101. For early examples of the notion that comity equals legal duty see *Warrender* v. *Warrender* (1835) 12 Ch. & F. 488 at p. 530: *not ex comitate sed ex debito justitiae*; *Watson* v. *Renton* (1792) 1 Bell's Cases 92, 102, cited by Nadelmann in *Jus et Lex, Festgabe für Gutzwiller* (1959), 263, at p. 275; Livermore, *Distinctions on the questions which arise from the Contrariety of the Positive Laws of different States and Nations* (New Orleans 1828); Gutzwiller, *Hague Rec.* 29 (1929 IV), pp. 340, 348; van Wesel, *Commentarii ad Novas Constitutiones*, Art. 13, n. 28: international legal duty; cp. Suyling, *De Statutentheorie in Nederland gedurende de 17de Eeuw* (1893), p. 52.

102. I. 3. 7.

103. See also *Praelectiones*, II. 1.3.1: "quamquam ipsa quaestio magis ad jus gentium quam ad jus civile pertineat quatenus quid diversi populi inter se servare debeant, ad juris gentium rationes pertinere manifestum est"; see also Meijers, *loc. cit.*, p. 668, note.

104. For the "tacit pact" of States see Grotius, *De jure belli ac pacis, Prolegomena*, 1, 15-17, 26, 40; Yntema, *op. cit.*, II, pp. 76, 81, 83, 84 and 85, n. 65. See also Kollewijn, *loc. cit.*, p. 133. But see Huber, *De iure civitatis*, III, 10, Nos. 1 and 2: "etsi non teneantur ex pacto vel necessitate subordinationis". And see Meijers, *loc. cit.*, p. 667, n. 2.

105. *Praelectiones*, II, 1.3.3.

106. Cp. Meijers, *loc. cit.*, at p. 670, citing in addition to *Praelectiones*, II, 1.3.3, *Heedendaegse Rechtsgelerthejt*, I. 3.8. and 10; Kollewijn above p. 123, n. 97, at pp. 145, 146, but see pp. 138, 142; Yntema, *Vom deutschen zum europäischen Recht*, II (1963), 65 at pp. 75 ff.; (1966), 65 *Mich.L.R.*, at pp. 19 ff.

107. This insight may prove helpful when the place of the doctrine of acquired rights in English and American law must be examined.

108. Sack in *Law, A Century of Progress*, III (1937), pp. 322 ff.; Gutzwiller, *Hague Rec.* 29 (1929 IV), pp. 332 ff.

109. The same applied to the Curia Regis, the Chancellor's court, the Star Chamber and the Council.

110. If it was unavoidable to consider foreign law, the experts in civil law were consulted.

111. See above sec. 5, No. 6, pp. 4-5.

112. *Dungannon* v. *Hackett* (1702), 1 Eq.Ca.Abr. 289; *Daws* v. *Pindar* (1675), 2 Mod. 45; *Blanskard* v. *Galdy* (1693), 4 Mod. 222; *Robinson* v. *Bland* (1760), 2 Burr. 1077; 1 W.Bl. 234, 256: contract; *Mostyn* v. *Fabrigas* (1774), 1 Cowp. 161, 171: tort; *Scrimshire* v. *Scrimshire* (1752), 2 Hag. Cons. 395: marriage; *Pipon* v. *Pipon* (1744), Amb. 25, 799; *Thorne* v. *Watkins* (1750), 2 Ves. sen 35: succession; *Solomon* v. *Ross* (1764), 1 H.Bl. 131; Wallis-Lyne, *Irish Chancery Reports* (1839), 59 n.; *Jollet* v. *Deponthieu* (1769), 1 H.Bl. 132 (n); *Neale* v. *Cottingham* (1770), 1 H.Bl. 132 n.; Wallis-Lyne, *Irish Chancery Rep.* (1839), 54: bankruptcy. As regards foreign judgments see *Walker* v. *Witter* (1771), 1 Doug. 1, 4.

113. Voet, Huber, Gail, Mynsinger and others; see Anton (1956), 5 *I.C.L.Q.*, 534, 538 ff.

114. (1775), 1 Cowp. 341, 343; see also Lord Stowell in *Dalrymple* v. *Dalrymple* (1811), 2 Hag. Con. 54.

115. At p. 343. Cp. *Harford* v. *Morris* (1776), 2 Hag. Ecc. 423, 430, 434. But see Lord Mansfield in *Robinson* v. *Bland* (1760), 1 W.Bl. 234, 246 (local, personal statutes).

116. See below, sec. 13, No. 22, pp. 23-25, for this aspect of the doctrine of acquired rights.

117. Jabez Henry, *The Judgment of the Court of Demarara in the case of Odwin v. Forbes, . . . To which is prefixed a Treatise on the Difference between Personal and Real Statutes and its Effects on Foreign Judgments, Contracts, Marriage and Wills*, XVI, 296 pp. (1823); see also de Nova, *Hague Rec.*, at p. 469. Clarke, *Summary of Colonial Laws* (1834); Burge, *Commentaries on Colonial and Foreign Laws generally, and in their Conflict with each other and with the Law of England* (1838): Wheaton, *Elements of International Law*, I (1836), p. 136; Reddie, *Inquiries in International Law* (1842); Hosack, *Treatise on the Conflict of Laws in England and Scotland* (1847); see Lorenzen (1934), 48 *Harv.L.R.*, 15, at p. 19; Harrison, *Clunet*, 1880, p. 429. Prater, *Cases illustrative of the Conflict of Laws between the Laws of England and Scotland* (1835); Dwarris, *General Treatise on Statutes* (1830-1831), Pt. II, pp. 647-665.

118. See the early cases cited by Nadelmann in *Ius et Lex, Festgabe für Gutzwiller*, 263, at p. 265.

119. Livermore, *Dissertations on the questions which arise from the Contrariety of Positive Laws of different States and Nations*, New Orleans, 1828, and the comments by De Nova (1964), 8 *Am. J. of Legal History*, 136; *Diritto internazionale*, 16 (1962), I. 207; Kent, *Commentaries on American Law*, 1826-1830; Story, *Commentaries on the Conflict of Laws, Foreign and Domestic, in regard to Contracts, Rights and Remedies, and especially in regard to Marriages, Divorces, Wills, Successions and Judgments* (1834), 2 ed. (1841), XXXIV and 927 ff.; see the comments by Lorenzen, 48 *Harv.L.R.*, 15 (1934), *Selected Articles* (1947), p. 181; *Rev.crit.d.i.p.*, 1935, 295; Nadelmann in *Jus et Lex, Festgabe für Gutzwiller* (1959), 263, at p. 272; (1966), 65 *Mich.L.R.*, 1; (1961), 5 *Am. J. of Legal History*, 230. See also Gardner, *Institutes of International Law*, public and private, as settled by the Supreme Court of the United States, New York, 1860.

120. Paras. 18, 20, 23. See Lorenzen (1923), 33 *Yale L.J.*, 736; (1934), 48 *Harv. L.R.*, 15, at p. 37; *Selected Articles*, p. 1, at p. 3, p. 181, at p. 199.

121. See Lorenzen (1923), 33 *Yale L.R.*, 736, at p. 740; (1934), 48 *Harv.L.R.*,

15, at p. 37; Selected Articles p. 1, at pp. 5 ff.; 181, at p. 201, but see the critique by Mann, *Hague Rec.* 111 (1964 I), 1, at pp. 31-33.

122. See also paras. 25, 33, 34, 35, 36, 38; see also Evrigenis, *loc. cit.*, at p. 326.

123. The conclusions of Mann, *Hague Rec.* 111 (1964 I), 1, at p. 33, are diametrically opposed, but it is believed that they treat Story's approach to the conflict of laws in isolation, torn out of its historical setting and in the light of rules of Public International Law which had not yet reached the stage of refinement imputed to them by Mann.

124. See below sects. 15-19, paras. 29-39, pp. 30-44.

125. See, e.g., *Huber* v. *Steiner*, (1835), 2 Bing N.C. 200, at p. 211; Savigny, *System des heutigen gemeinen Rechts*, 8 (1849), p. 25 n. *(a)*; Fœlix, *Traité de droit international privé*, (1843) ss. 9-11.

126. Gutzwiller, *Hague Rec.* 29 (1929 IV), p. 337, with lit. n. 3.

127. Gutzwiller, *ibid.*, p. 337, n. 4.

128. *Archiv für die zivilistische Praxis*, 24 (1841), pp. 230-311 (cited as Wächter, I), 25 (1842), pp. 150-200; 361-491 (cited as Wächter, II); see Nadelmann (1964), 13 *Am.J.Comp.L.*, 414; De Nova, *Hague Rec.* 118 (1966 II), 437, at pp. 452-456; and cp. Wengler (1961), 28 *Law & Contemp. Problems*, 822, 829, n. 31; Baade, *ibid.*, p. 675, n. 9, as regards Wächter's influence on Currie.

129. I, 280 and notes 94-98 (lit.).

130. I, 286.

131. I, pp. 274, 275, n. 81 (lit.), 256-257: "Der neue Sprachgebrauch dagegen, der sich allmählig, ohne dass man Abweichung von Aelteren betrachtet zu haben scheint, bildete ist ein ganz anderer. *Statuta personalia* sind nach ihm die sämtlichen Gesetze welche am Wohnort einer Person gelten, von welchem Gegenstand, ob von Personen, Sachen oder Formen eines Geschäftes sie handeln mögen, *statuta realia*, das Recht welches am Orte gilt wo eine gewisse Sache liegt, *statuta mixta* das Recht welches am Orte gilt wo eine gewisse Handlung vorfiel."

132. I, 287-288, 307, 310; II, 378.

133. I, 287, 290, 292.

134. I, 292.

135. I, 299, 304, 310-311; II, 162.

136. I, 300-301 and n. 145; II, 391.

137. I, 301; II, 162, 170.

138. I, 299 ff., especially pp. 301, 302-303 citing Maurenbrecher, *Deutsches Privatrecht* (2 ed.), I, 315: "die Regierung muss den Status des Fremden schützen so gut wie ihre Personen und ihre Vermögen, so weit sie diese überhaupt als wohlerworbene Rechte bei sich anerkannt . . ."

139. I, p. 236-237: "Rechtsverhältnis welches entweder im Auslande begründet wurde oder bei welchem Ausländer beteiligt sind, oder welches sonst mit dem Auslande in einer Beziehung steht." For the background of this approach see Steindorff, *Sachnormen im Internationalen Privatrecht* (1958), 42.

140. I, 237, 261, 264-266; II, 162.

141. I, 239-241, 267, 268.

142. I, 242, 255, 267, 268; II, 170, 180, n. 302.

143. I, 262, 264, 268; II, 362, 364, 385, 387.

144. I, p. 266; II, 405.

145. II, 362 (property relations between spouses, personal statute), p. 364 (succession—real statutes); pp. 384-386 (movables—real statutes).

146. I, 310.

147. *System des heutigen Römischen Rechts*, 8 (1849); for lit. see Gutzwiller, *Der Einfluss Savigny's auf die Entwicklung des Internationalprivatrechts* (1923); *Hague Rec.* 29 (1929 IV), pp. 352 ff., Neuhaus, *Rabels Z.*, 15 (1949), pp. 364-381;

Yntema (1952), 2 *A.J.Comp.L.*, 297, 309; Maridakis in *Festschrift für Lewald* (1953), 309; Coing, *Eranion Maridakis*, III (1964), 19; De Nova, *Hague Rec.* 118 (1966 II), 437, 456-464.

148. Savigny, pp. 2, 122 ff.

149. P. 25.

150. P. 132, para. 361 (5).

151. See above, p. 132; cp. Savigny, p. 127.

152. "Völkerrechtliche Gemeinschaft der mit einander verkehrenden Nationen", see Savigny, pp. 28, 118.

153. "Dass bei jedem Rechtsverhältnis dasjenige Recht aufgesucht wurde welchem dieses Rechtsverhältnis seiner eigentümlichen Art nach angehört oder unterworfen ist"; see Savigny, p. 27.

154. Neuhaus, *loc. cit.*, 364, at p. 371.

155. Cp. Neuhaus, *loc. cit.*, 364, 368.

156. See von Bar, *Theorie und Praxis des internationalen Privatrechts*, I (2 ed. 1889), 107.

157. See below sec. 27, Nos. 56-58, pp. 95-98.

158. Neuhaus, *loc. cit.*, p. 366: "auf der Kopernikanischen Wende in der Fragestellung von einer schematischen Klassifizierung der Gesetze zur individualisierenden Suche nach dem natürlichen 'Sitz' jedes einzelnen Rechtsverhältnisses".

159. *Private International Law* (1858).

160. (1890), 6 *L.Q.R.*, 1; (1891), 7 *L.Q.R.*, 113; *Conflict of Laws* (1 ed. 1894).

161. (1775), 1 Cowp. 341, 343; see above p. 18.

162. (1890), 6 *L.Q.R.*, 1, at pp. 3, 4, 6, 12, 13, 18, 20, 21; *Conflict of Laws* (3 ed. 1922), pp. 3, 4, 6, 7, 13, 14, 20.

163. (1890), 6 *L.Q.R.*, 10, 11, 13.

164. Horst Müller, *Der Grundsatz der Wohlerworbenen Rechte im internationalen Privatrecht* (1935), reviewed by Gutzwiller, *Rabels Z.*, 10 (1936), 1056.

165. See Gutzwiller, *loc. cit.*

166. (1775), 1 Cowp. 341, 343; see above, p. 18.

167. Wächter, *Archiv für die zivilistische Praxis*, 24 (1841), 230, at p. 300 and note 146; 25 (1842), 361, at p. 391; Savigny, *System des heutigen Römischen Rechts* (1849), para. 361 (5), p. 132, Guthrie's transl. (2 ed. 1880), pp. 147 ff.; Lorenzen (1924) 33 *Yale L.J.* 736, *Selected Articles* (1947) 1; W. W. Cook (1924) 33 *Yale L.J.* 457, *The Logical and Legal Basis of the Conflict of Laws* (1942) 1; Arminjon, *Hague Rec.* 44 (1933 II) 1; Caswell (1959), 8 *I.C.L.Q.*, 268, at pp. 285-286.

168. For details see Nadelmann, in *Ius et Lex, Festgabe für Gutzwiller* (1959), 263, at pp. 276-279; Yntema in *Festschrift für Rabel*, I (1953), 513, at p. 526, n. 29; Lipstein [1972 B], 31 *Cambridge L.J.*, 67-71.

169. 1 ed. (1880), p. 288, and note 1; Dicey, *Conflict of Laws* (3 ed. 1922), pp. 3, 5, notes.

170. Nadelmann, *loc. cit.* (above n. 168), 277, 278; for the revision of these references in subsequent editions see Nadelmann, p. 277, note 90, and p. 278.

171. *Praelectiones*, II, 1.3.3; see above p. 15 and n. 105.

172. Dicey, *Conflict of Laws* (3 ed. 1922), pp. 23, 27; see also (1891), 7 *L.Q.R.*, 113, at p. 118. It was only the last step in the logical argument when the editors of the sixth edition (1949), pp. 11, 12, replaced the qualification that the right must have been "duly" acquired by the requirement that it must have been acquired "according to the English rules of the conflict of laws". For comments see Falconbridge (1950), 66 *L.Q.R.*, 104, 106; Mann (1949), 12 *M.L.R.*, 518, 520; Cavers (1950), 63 *Harv.L.R.*, 1278, 1280; Rheinstein (1950), 35 *N.Y.U.L.R.*, 180, 181.

173. (1891), 7 *L.Q.R.*, 113, 118; *Conflict of Laws* (3 ed. 1922), p. 33.

174. See above p. 23.

175. Cp. Dicey, *Conflict of Laws* (3 ed. 1922), pp. 26, 27; (1891), 7 *L.Q.R.*, 113, 115.

176. Arminjon, *loc. cit.*, p. 39.

177. See below, sec. 16, No. 31, pp. 32-36.

177a. Switzerland excepted.

178. See above p. 15. For some modern views on comity see Cardozo J. in *Loucks* v. *Standard Oil* (1918), 224 N.Y. 99, 111, 120, N.E. 198, 201-202; *Dean* v. *Dean*, 241 N.Y. 240, 243; 149 N.E. 844, 846 (1924); Cheatham (1948), 51 *Harv.L.R.*, 361, 376 n. 39.

179. Below sec. 21, Nos. 41-42, pp. 63-66.

180. *A Treatise on the Conflict of Laws*, I (1935), para. 42.1, p. 274, para. 5.4, p. 53; III, pp. 1968, 1972; (1896), 10 *Harv.L.R.*, 168, at 170; and see the comments by de Sloovère (1936), 13 *N.Y.U.L.R.*, 333, 338, 342, 345; McClintock (1936), 84 *U.Pa.L.R.*, 309; Cook (1935), 35 *Col.L.R.*, 1154; Read (1935), 49 *Harv.L.R.*, 346, 347; Cheshire (1936), 52 *L.Q.R.*, 540; Falconbridge (1935), 13 *Can. Bar Rev.*, 531, 533; Rheinstein in *Festschrift für Rabel*, I (1954), 539, 585-586.

181. See, e.g., as to contracts, *Treatise*, II, para. 322.4; torts, *Treatise*, II, para. 378.1. And see Cavers, *The Choice of Law Process* (1965), pp. 6-7.

182. Cp. Beach (1917-1918), 27 *Yale L.J.*, 656-667, but see Taney C.J. in *Bank of Augusta* v. *Earle*, 13 Pet. 519, 589, 10 L.Ed. 274, 308 (1839).

183. See p. 25.

184. No. 38, p. 43.

185. Rheinstein, *Festschrift für Rabel*, I (1954), 539-589; (1954-1955), 22 *U.Chi.L.R.*, 775-824; Cheatham (1953-1954), 28 *Vanderbilt L.R.*, 581; Cook, *Logical and Legal Basis*, p. 41; see *Commercial Travellers* v. *Wolfe* (1947), 331 US 586 91 L.Ed. 1687; *Alaska Packers Association* v. *Industrial Accident Comm'n*, 294 US 532 (1933); *Richards* v. *US*, 369 US 1 1962; *Clay* v. *Sun Insurance etc.*, 377 US 179 (1964); *Hughes* v. *Fetter*, 341 US 609 (1951); *Allendorf* v. *Elgin, etc., Ry*, 8 Ill. 2d. 164, 133 N.E. (2d) 288 (1956); *Wells* v. *Simon Abrasive Co.*, 345 US 514 (1953); *Watson* v. *Employers, etc.*, 348 US 66 (1954); foreign law: *Home Ins. Co.* v. *Dick*, 281 US 397 (1930); de Sloovère (1935-1936), 13 *N.Y.U.L.R.*, 333 at p. 354 and notes 92, 93; Beach (1917-1918), 27 *Yale L.J.*, 565, at p. 662, 665; *Bond* v. *Hume*, 243 US 15, 21 (1916); Jackson (1945), 45 *Col.L.R.*, 1; Weintraub (1958-1959), 44 *Iowa L.R.*, 449; Ehrenzweig, *P.I.L.*, p. 63, n. 2, p. 34; Bernstein, *N.J.W.* 1965, 2273.

186. (1924), 33 *Yale L.J.*, 736; *Selected Articles* (1947), pp. 1 ff. See also Goodrich (1950), 50 *Col.L.R.* 881-899; Harper (1947), 56 *Yale L.J.*, 1055-1077.

187. See below No. 41, pp. 63-64

188. Cook, *The Logical and Legal Basis of the Conflict of Laws* (1942), 1 ff., at pp. 20-22; (1924), 33 *Yale L.J.*, 457 at pp. 475, 489; (1943), 21 *Can. Bar Rev.*, 249; (1943), 37 *Ill.L.R.*, 418; for comments see Rheinstein (1943), 10 *U.Chi.L.R.*, 446; Cavers (1943), 56 *Harv.L.R.*, 1170; Lorenzen (1943), 52 *Yale L.J.*, 680; Hancock (1944), 44 *Col.L.R.*, 579 = (1944), 5 *U. of Toronto L.R.*, 476; Cheatham (1944), 93 *U.Pa.L.R.*, 112; (1945), 58 *Harv.L.R.*, 366, at pp. 386-387; Keith (1943), 59 *L.Q.R.*, 378; Morris, *ibid.*, p. 379; Falconbridge (1943), 21 *Can. Bar Rev.*, 329 = (1943), 37 *Ill.L.R.*, 375; see also Lorenzen (1924), 33 *Yale L.J.*, 736, *Selected Articles* (1947), p. 1 ff.; in (1943), 52 *Yale L.J.*, 680, 681, he traces the doctrine back to Hohfeld (1909), 9 *Col.L.R.*, 492, (1910), *ibid.*, 283, 520.

189. At pp. 20-21.

190. See the words of Cardozo J. in *Loucks* v. *Standard Oil Co.* (above, p. 139, n. 178), para. 4: "A foreign statute is not law in this state ... No law can exist as such except the law of the land but ... vested rights shall be protected."

191. Monaco, *L'efficacia della legge nello spazio* (2 ed. 1964), para. 13, pp. 28-31, and note 1 with lit. See also Ehrenzweig, *P.I.L.*, p. 61.

192. Monaco, *loc. cit.*, p. 30 and note 2; Ago, *Teoria del diritto internazionale privato* (1934), pp. 99-100; *Hague Rec.* (1936 IV) 243, pp. 294 ff., at 301 ff., 304; *Lezioni di diritto internazionale privato* (1939), p. 73 ff.; Maury, *Hague Rec.* 57 (1936 III), 325, at pp. 381-383; Sperduti, *Saggi di teoria generale del diritto internazionale privato* (1967), pp. 91-95; Bernadini, *Produzione di norme giuridiche mediante rinvio* (1966), *passim.*

193. Except for the answer to the question whether the correctness of the application of foreign law by a lower court can be the object of an appeal on points of law only; see Zaytay, *Contribution à l'étude de la condition de la loi étrangère en droit international privé français*, pp. 163-173, *idem* in *Anwendung ausländischen Rechts im international Privatrecht* (Dierk Müller ed., 1968), pp. 193-213; Ç. David, *La loi étrangère devant le juge du fond* (1965), p. 195, No. 258.

194. Cavers (1950), 63 *Harv.L.R.*, 822-832.

195. *Guiness* v. *Miller*, 291 F. 769, 770 (S.D.N.Y. 1923); see also *Direktion der Diskontogesellschaft* v. *U.S. Steel Corporation*, 300 F. 741 (S.D.N.Y. 1924); *Louis-Dreyfus* v. *Paterson Steamship Ltd.*, 43 F. (2d) 824 (C.C.A. 2. Circ. 1930); *Siegmann* v. *Meyer*, 100 F. (2d) 367 (2 Circ. 1938).

196. *Della nazionalità come fondamento del diritto delle genti* (1851); see also *Clunet* 1 (1874), pp. 221, 285; see Sereni, *The Italian Conception of International Law* (1943), pp. 160-181; de Nova (1963), 28 *Law and Contemporary Problems*, 808; Nadelmann (1969), 17 *Am.J.Comp.L.*, 418.

197. Contrast the approach to the same question by English law in the 19th century: Sinclair (1950), 27 *British Year Book of International Law*, 125, at pp. 131-137; Mervyn Jones (1956), 5 *International and Comparative Law Quarterly*, 230, at p. 243; Parry, *Hague Rec.* 90 (1956 III), at pp. 704-705.

198. *Udny* v. *Udny* (1866), L.R. 1, Sc. & Div. 441.

199. Such rules would be described today as spatially conditioned rules of domestic law or as rules *d'application immédiate*—see below sec. 28, No. 59.

200. Pillet, *Principes* (1903), pp. 265 ff.

201. See below sec. 17, Nos. 33-34.

202. Zitelmann, *Internationales Privatrecht*, I (1899); *Festgabe für Karl Bergbohm* (1919), 207 = *Diritto Internazionale*, 15 (1961), I, 152; Frankenstein, *Internationales Privatrecht*, I (1926); Briggs (1953), 6 *Vanderbilt L.R.*, 667, 707; (1955), 39 *Minn.L.R.*, 517; (1955), 4 *Int. and Comp. L.Q.*, 329; (1948), 61 *Harv.L.R.*, 1165; (1945), 15 *Miss.L.J.*, 77; and see the comments by Cavers, *The Choice of Law Process* (1965), pp. 211-273; Sohn (1942), 55 *Harv.L.R.*, 978, 982, 1003.

203. For a survey see *Hague Rec.* 124 (1968 II), 170-173.

204. *Treatise on the Conflict of Laws* (1962); *Private International Law* (1967), 93; *Specific Principles of Private Transnational Law*, Hague Rec. 124 (1968 II), 170.

205. *Hague Rec., loc. cit.*, at pp. 214-215; 255-260; (1963), 28 *Law & Contemporary Problems*, 700; *Treatise*, pp. 352-353.

206. Ehrenzweig, Proposition 3; see also *Hague Rec.*, pp. 200-213.

207. Ehrenzweig, Proposition 6.

208. Ehrenzweig, Proposition 7.

209. Ehrenzweig, Proposition 1.

210. See Ehrenzweig, *P.I.L.*, ss. 33, 138. From these it would appear that in practice courts interpret the intention of the parties as if this concerned a pure question of fact, although the intention of the parties may have been expressed and intended to be understood in the light of some foreign system of law. Such a conclusion overlooks the need to interpret words in the light of a foreign language

and of their meaning in foreign law: *Studd* v. *Cook* (1883), 8 App. Cas. 577, 600, 604.

211. Ehrenzweig, Proposition 2.

212. Ehrenzweig, Proposition 4.

213. Ehrenzweig, Proposition 5.

214. Ehrenzweig, *Treatise* (1962), 465-490.

215. Above No. 19, pp. 20-21.

216. See above p. 11.

217. See, e.g., *Pugh* v. *Pugh* [1951], p. 482.

218. Ehrenzweig (1963), 28 *Law & Contemporary Problems*, 700, 703.

219. Above No. 6, pp. 4-5.

220. E.g., contracts: R.S.C., O. 11, Rule 1 (1) (f); torts: R.S.C., O. 11, Rule 1 (1) (h).

221. For their analysis see below Part III, Nos. 53-63, pp. 93-104.

222. See below sec. 21, Nos. 41-43, pp. 63-67.

223. See Rheinstein in *Festschrift für Rabel*, I (1954), 569-589; W. B. Cowles, *Nordisk Tidschrift for international Ret*, 31 (1951), 51; Brainerd Currie, *Selected Essays on the Conflict of Laws* (1963), 188-360, 445-583; for surveys of the practice see 74 *A.L.R.*, 710; 100 *A.L.R.*, 1143; 134 *A.L.R.*, 1472; 137 *A.L.R.*, 965; annotation in 95 L. ed. 1212; Baxter (1963), 16 *Stanford L.R.*, 1 and the lit. cited by Cavers, *Choice of Law Process* (1965), 117, n. 3.

See also Dodd (1926), 39 *Harv.L.R.*, 533; Ross (1931), 15 *Minn.L.R.*, 161; Lorenzen, *Rec. Gény* III (1934), 437; Cheatham (1944), 44 *Col.L.R.*, 330; Jackson (1945), 45 *Col.L.R.*, 1; Freund (1946), 49 *Harv.L.R.*, 1210; Cheatham (1953), 6 *Vanderbilt L.R.*, 581; Hart (1954), 54 *Col.L.R.*, 489; Hill (1958), 53 *N.W.L.R.*, 427, 541; Weintraub (1959), 44 *Iowa L.R.*, 449; Leflar (1963), 28 *Law & Contemp. Problems*, 706; Horowitz (1967), 14 *U.C.L.A.L.R.*, 1191; Cavers, *Hague Rec.* 131 (1973 III), 77, 108-121; Martin (1976), 61 *Cornell L.R.*, 185; Ehrenzweig, *Private International Law* III (1977), 6 (34); Weintraub (1977), 41 *Law & Contemp. Problems*, (No. 2), 104; Hertz (1977), 27 *U.Tor.L.J.*, 1.

224. Rheinstein, *loc. cit.*, pp. 541, 547, 555, 559, i.e., the 14th Amendment (due process of law); art. IV s. 1 of the Constitution (Full Faith and Credit) and art. 1, s. 10 (1) of the Constitution (contract clause).

225. Rheinstein, *passim*; *Klaxon* v. *Stentor Electric Manufacturing Co.*, 313 US 487, 85 L.ed. 1447 (1941); *Griffin* v. *McCoach*, 313 US 498, 85 L.ed. 1481 (1941); for the approach to conflict rules in a federal court see *Richards* v. *US*, 369 US 1, 12; 7 L.ed. 2d 492, 500 (1962).

226. Above, note 225.

227. *Klaxon* v. *Stentor*, above n. 225, at p. 497. It did so, nevertheless, when it posited the application of the law of procedure and evidence of the forum on the ground that these matters are subject to the *lex fori*: *Hawkins* v. *Barney's Lessee*, 5 Pet. 457, 466, 467, 8 L.ed. 190, 193, 194 (1831); *McElmoyle* v. *Cohen*, 13 Pet. 312, 324, 325, 10 L.ed. 177, 183, 185 (1839) and *(obiter) Home Insurance Co.* v. *Dick*, 281 US 397, 407, 74 L.ed. 926, 933 (1930); *Wells* v. *Simonds Abrasive Co.*, 345 US 514, 516, 517, 97 L.ed. 1211, 1215 (1953); *Order of United Commercial Travelers* v. *Wolfe*, 331 US 586, 607, 91 L.ed. 1687, 1700 (1947).

And see now *Day & Zimmermann* v. *Hawley K. Challoner*, 423 U.S. 3, 46 L.ed. 3 (1975) on *certiorari* from 512 F. 2d 77 (5 Cir. 1975). It may be noted in passing that the Circuit Court's disregard of the Cambodian *lex loci delicti* is justified by the rule that an army of occupation is not subject to the local law: Dicey and Morris, *Conflict of Laws* (8 ed. 1973), 244 with cases.

228. Rheinstein, pp. 580-581.

229. *Alaska Packers Ass.* v. *Industrial Accident Commission*, 294 US 532, 544,

546, 547, 79 L.ed. 1044, 1050, 1051, 1052 (1935); *Pink* v. *A.A.A. Highway Express*, 314 US 201, 209, 86 L.ed. 152, 158 (1941); *Pacific Employers Ins. Co.* v. *Industrial Accident Commission*, 306 US 493, 500, 83 L.ed. 940, 944 (1939); *Magnolia Petroleum Co.* v. *Hunt*, 320 US 430, 436, 88 L.ed. 149, 154 (1943); *Bradford Electric Co.* v. *Clapper*, 286 US 145, 156, 76 L.ed. 1026, 1033 (1932); Rheinstein 583; *Re Crichton*, 20 N.Y. 2d 124, 228 N.E. 2d 789, 281 N.Y.S. 2d 811 (1967).

230. *Alaska Packers Ass.* v. *Industrial Accident Commission* (above n. 229), at p. 538.

231. At p. 542; Cavers, *The Choice of Law Process* (1965), p. 105; De Nova, 28 *Law & Contemporary Problems* (1963), 808, 818-820.

232. Rheinstein, *loc. cit.*, pp. 573-575, 547, 552, 554. The problem as to when a right has been acquired was more difficult. Beale (above No. 24, p. 26) solved it by a doctrinal approach, and the US Supreme Court did so, too, in a few decisions by the application of abstract and rigid choice of law rules; *lex loci delicti: Western Union Telegraph* v. *Chiles*, 214 US 274; 53 L.ed. 994 (1909); *Western Union* v. *Brown*, 234 US 542, 58 L.ed. 1457 (1913); see also *Slater* v. *Mexican Railways*, 194 US 120, 48 L.ed. 900 (1904); *lex loci contractus: N.Y. Life Insurance Co.* v. *Dodge*, 246 US 357, 62 L.ed. 772 (1918); *Mutual Life Ins. Co.* v. *Liebing*, 259 US 209, 66 L.ed. 900 (1922); *Hartford Accident and Indemnity Co.* v. *Delta Pine*, 292 US 134, 78 L.ed. 1178 (1934).

In other cases the exercise of territorial jurisdiction was believed to be concentrated on persons and events within the territorial reach: see p. 33, n. 236 and see *Bradford Electric Co.* v. *Clapper* (above n. 229) at p. 184 (per Stone J. diss.): "The Full Faith and Credit clause has not hitherto been thought to do more than compel recognition outside the state of operation and effect of its laws upon persons and events within it."

233. Rheinstein, pp. 555-567; for the contract clause (US Const., art. I, s. 10 (1)) in a conflict of laws in time see *Watson* v. *Employers Liability Ass. Corp.*, 348 US 66, 70, 90 L.ed. 74, 81 (1954); for the foreign commerce clause (U.S. Const., art. 8 (3)) see *Fuss* v. *French National Railroads* 35 Misc. 2d 680, 231 N.Y.S. 2d 57 (1962).

234. *Hughes* v. *Fetter*, 341 US 609, 612, 613; 95 L.ed. 1212 (1951).

235. *Pink* v. *A.A.A. Highways Express*, at pp. 209-210; *Alaska Packers Ass.* v. *Industrial Accident Commission*, at pp. 546, 548; *Milwaukee County* v. *White*, 296 US 268, 273, 274, 80 L.ed. 220, 225, 226 (1935); *Order of United Commercial Travelers* v. *Wolfe*, at p. 607; *Broderick* v. *Rosner*, 294 US 629, 642, 70 L.ed. 1100, 1107 (1935).

236. *Pacific Employers Ins. Co.* v. *Industrial Accident Commission*, at p. 502; *Watson* v. *Employers Liability Assn. Co.*, 348 US 66, 73, 99 L.ed. 74, 82; *Clay* v. *Sun Ins. Office*, 377 US 179, 181, 12 L.ed. 229, 231 (1964).

237. *Magnolia Petroleum Co.* v. *Hunt*, at p. 436; further developed in *International Commission of Wisconsin* v. *McCartin* 330 U.S. 622, 91 L. 2d 1140 (1947); see also *Bradford Electric Co.* v. *Clapper*, at p. 156; *Quong Ham Wah Co.* v. *Industrial Accident Commission*, 255 US 445, 65 L.ed. 723 (1921).

238. *Milwaukee County* v. *White* (above n. 235), at pp. 276, 277; *Hoopeston Canning Co.* v. *Callen*, 318 US 313, 87 L.ed. 777 (1943); *Alaska Packers Ass.* v. *Industrial Accident Comm.*, 294 US 532, 79 L.ed. 1044.

239. *Broderick* v. *Rosner* (above p. 33, n. 235), at pp. 642, 643.

240. *Bradford Electric* v. *Clapper*, at p. 162.

241. *Alaska Packers Ass.* v. *Industrial Accident Commission* (above p. 33, n. 229), at pp. 542, 549; *Hartford Accident and Indemnity Co.* v. *Delta Pine Land Co.*, 292 US 143, 150, 78 L.ed. 1178, 1181 (1934); *Carroll* v. *Lanza*, 349 US 408, 99 L.ed. 1183 (1955); *Vanston Bondholders Protective Committee* v. *Green*, 329

US 156, 161, 162, 91 L.ed. 162, 165, 166 (1946); *Richards* v. *US*, 369 US 1, 15, 7 L.ed. 2d 492, 501 (1962).

242. *Watson* v. *Employers Liability Assur. Corp.*, 348 US 66, 72, 99 L.ed. 74 82 (1954); *Osborn* v. *Ozlin*, 310 US 53, 84 L.ed. 1074 (1940).

243. *Converse* v. *Hamilton*, 224 US 243, 260, 56 L.ed. 749, 755 (1911); *Griffin* v. *McCoach*, 313 US 498, 503, 506, 85 L.ed. 1481, 1445, 1456 (1941); such as: *Bond* v. *Hume*, 243 US 15, 21, 61 L.ed. 565, 567 (1917); imputing capacity to contract to a married woman contrary to the *lex fori*: *Union Trust* v. *Grosman*, 245 US 412, 62 L.ed. 368 (1918); doing a prohibited act in the country of the forum: *Bothwell* v. *Buckbee Mears & Co.*, 275 US 274, 278, 72 L.ed. 277, 280 (1927); enforcing penal law: *Huntington* v. *Altrill*, 146 US 657, 16 L.ed. 1123 (1892); *Hughes* v. *Fetter* (above p. 33, n. 234), at p. 612; *Order of Commercial Travelers of America* v. *Wolfe* (above p. 33, n. 227) at p. 624; *Home Insurance Co.* v. *Dick*, 281 US 397, 410, 74 L.ed. 926, 934 (1930); *Bradford Electric Co.* v. *Clapper* (above p. 33, n. 229), at p. 157; *Hartford Accident and Indemnity Co.* v. *Delta Pine Land Co.* (above n. 241) at p. 149.

The term recalls a similar phrase (manifestly against public policy) employed by the Hague Conventions on Private International Law.

244. *Home Insurance Co.* v. *Dick* (above n. 243)—an international claim not subject to the Full Faith and Credit Clause, but see also *John Hancock Mutual Life Ins. Co.* v. *Yates*, 299 US 178, 81 L.ed. 106, at p. 182 (1936); *Hartford Accident and Indemnity Co.* v. *Delta and Pine Land Co.* (above p. 34, n. 241), at p. 149; *Watson* v. *Employers Liability Assur. Corp.*, 348 US 66, 71, 88 L.ed. 76, 81 (1954).

245. *Hughes* v. *Fetter* (above p. 33, n. 234), at p. 617 (per Frankfurter, Reed, Jackson, Minton JJ. diss.); see also *Alaska Packers Ass.* v. *Industrial Accident Commission* (above p. 33, n. 229), at p. 541; *Carroll* v. *Lanza*, 349 US 408 at 412, 419, 99 L.ed. 1183, 1188, 1192 (1955), per Frankfurter diss.

246. *Pacific Employers Ins. Co.* v. *Industrial Accident Commission* (above p. 33, n. 229), at p. 502, but see the restriction imposed upon the alleged principle at p. 503; *Griffin* v. *McCoach* (above p. 32, n. 225), at p. 506; *Bradford Electric Company* v. *Clapper* (above p. 33, n. 229), at pp. 159, 164; *Hartford Accident and Indemnity Co.* v. *Delta Pine Land Co.* (above p. 34, n. 241), at p. 149.

247. See the statement in *Magnolia Petroleum Co.* v. *Hunt* (above p. 33, n. 229), at p. 436; *Clay* v. *Sun Ins. Office*, 377 US 179, 181, 12 L.ed. 229, 231 (1964).

248. Thus the plaintiff's substantive rights are not impaired: *Hughes* v. *Fetter* (above p. 33, n. 234), at p. 617 (diss.); *Alaska Packers Ass.* v. *Industrial Accident Commission* (above p. 33, n. 229), at p. 540.

249. *Bradford Electric Co.* v. *Clapper* (above p. 33, n. 229), at p. 159.

250. Above p. 34, and note 241.

251. *John Hancock Mutual Life Ins. Co.* v. *Yates* (above n. 244), at p. 183. For this term see Cavers, *The Choice of Law Process* (1965), p. 82, and n. 44.

252. See Frankfurter J. diss. in *Carroll* v. *Lanza*, 349 US 408 at pp. 416 ff., 99 L.ed. 1183, 1191 (1955).

Tort, survival of actions: *Hughes* v. *Fetter* (above p. 33, n. 234); Workmen's Compensation: *Alaska Packers Ass.* v. *Industrial Accident Commission* (above p. 33, n. 229); *Pacific Employers Ins. Co.* v. *Industrial Accident Commission* (above p. 33, n. 229); *Bradford Electric Co.* v. *Clapper* (above p. 33, n. 229);

Contract: *John Hancock Mutual Life Ins. Co.* v. *Yates* (above p. 34, n. 244); *Griffin* v. *McCoach* (above p. 34, n. 243); *Home Ins. Co.* v. *Dick* (above p. 34, n. 243); *Bradford Electric Co.* v. *Clapper* (above p. 33, n. 229) at p. 158; *Alaska Packers Ass.* v. *Industrial Accident Commission* (above p. 33, n. 229); *Pacific*

Employers Ins. Co. v. *Industrial Accident Commission* (above p. 33, n. 229) at p. 503;

Companies: *Pink* v. *A.A.A. Highways Express* (above p. 33, n. 229); *Order of United Commercial Travelers of America* v. *Wolfe* (above p. 33, n. 235); *Broderick* v. *Rosner* (above p. 33, n. 235); *Converse* v. *Hamilton* (above p. 34, n. 243);

For the problem of characterising contracts and torts see *Alaska Packers* v. *Industrial Accident Commission* (above p. 33, n. 229) at p. 542; *Broderick* v. *Rosner* (above p. 33, n. 235) at p. 644; *John Hancock Mutual Life Ins. Co.* v. *Yates* (above p. 34, n. 244) at p. 182; *Home Ins. Co.* v. *Dick* (above p. 34, n. 243) at p. 407.

The problem arose as a preliminary question in *Pink* v. *A.A.A. Highway Express* (above p. 33, n. 229).

253. Cp. Rheinstein (1962), 11 *Am.J.Comp.L.*, 632, 633.

254. *Selected Essays in the Conflict of Laws* (1963), 120-21, 171-172, 182-184, 188-189, 609. The literature is enormous. See also, e.g., de Nova, *Hague Rec.* 118 (1966 II), 591-606, with lit. p. 590, n. 1-3; Shapira, *The Interest Approach to Choice of Law* (1970); Kegel, *Hague Rec.* 112 (1964 II), pp. 95-207, Baxter (1963), 16 *Stanf. L.R.*, 1; Currie (1963), 28 *Law & Contemp. Problems*, 754, Ehrenzweig (1966), 80 *Harv.L.R.*, 377; Leflar (1966), 41 *N.Y.U.L.R.* 267; Westen (1967), 55 *Calif.L.R.*, 74. Juenger (1967), 118 *U.Pa.L.R.*, 202, Jayme *Rabel's Z.*, 38 (1974), 593; von Mehren (1974-75), 88 *Harv.L.R.*, 347; id. (1975), *Cornell L.R.*, 927; id. (1977), 41 *Law & Contemp. Problems*, 27; Shapira (1977) 77 *Col.L.R.*, 248; Lorenz, *Zur Struktur des I.P.R.* (1977); von Mehren (1978), 26 *Am.J.Comp.L.*, 31 (Suppl.).

255. See, e.g., Cavers, *Choice of Law Process* (1965), pp. 167, 89; Morris, *Conflict of Laws* (1971), pp. 542 ff., 490.

256. In Europe unilateral choice of law rules and spatially conditioned internal rules serve this purpose. For the various techniques see below No. 59, pp. 99-102.

257. If one of the possible systems involved shows a governmental interest to be applied in the circumstances, that legal system must be applied. If several show a concurrent interest, the *lex fori* takes over; it is the same, if no legal system shows an interest.

258. *Archiv für die zivilistische Praxis*, 24 (1841), 299, 304; 310-311; *ibid.*, 25 (1842), 162.

259. 12 N.Y. 2d 473, 191 N.E. 2d 279 (1963).

See (1935-36), 1 *Univ. of Toronto L.J.*, 358, 365-66; Linden (1962), 40 *Can.Bar Rev.*, 284, 286 n. 66; Rosenberg (1967), 67 *Col.L.R.*, 459; Trautman *ibid.*, 465, 466 ff, 469; Reese (1971), 71 *ibid.*, 548, 554 n. 2; (1972), 57 *Cornell L.R.*, 315, 318; (1977), 16 *Col.J.Int.L.*, 1, 7; Isakoff (1977), 77 *Col.L.R.*, 272, 275 n. 69; Shapira *ibid.*, 262 n. 69, 270.

260. See below Nos. 36-39, pp. 41-44.

261. Fränkel, *Rabels Z.*, 4 (1930), 239; see also Cavers (1933), 47 *Harv.L.R.*, 173.

262. Above, p. 6.

263. Cavers, *Choice of Law Process* (1965), pp. 76, 8, 9, esp. 76, 113, 122; *Hague Rec.* 131 (1970 III), 75-308.

264. *Ibid.*, pp. 137, 200, 215.

265. *Ibid.*, p. 15.

266. Cp. as regards German law, EGBGB, art. 12.

267. *Ibid.*, pp. 134, 136, 142, 150. For a discussion of any preference between the two see p. 156.

268. See above, pp. 36-37 with lit., esp. Cavers, p. 89.

269. Cavers, pp. 89, 98, 100-101, but see p. 171.

270. Cavers, pp. 120, 124; the *lex fori* must determine it: *ibid.*, pp. 106, 218-219; *Hague Rec.* 131 (1970 III), pp. 75-308.

271. Cavers, p. 222.

272. Cavers, p. 139; the personal law of the plaintiff does not seem to attract attention, possibly on the irrelevant ground of lack of jurisdiction of the plaintiff's State. For the meaning of "home State" see Cavers, p. 154. Neither is the question taken into account as to the burden of proof of all these rules taken from different legal systems.

273. Cavers, p. 146.

274. Cavers, p. 153.

275. Cavers, pp. 156-157, but see 49 *Texas L.R.* 211, 217 (1971).

276. Cavers, p. 159; this principle expresses the rule in *Schmidt* v. *Driscoll Hotel Inc.*, 249 Minn. 376, 82 N.W.Ld. 365 (1957)—for meaning of "special controls" see p. 164.

277. Cavers, pp. 160-162.

278. Cavers, p. 166. This principle expresses the rule in *Babcock* v. *Jackson*, 12 N.Y. 2d 473, 482, 191 N.E. 2d 279, 284 (1963); *Haumschild* v. *Continental Casualty Co.*, 7 Wis. 2d 130, 95 N.W. 2d 814 (1959). Cavers stresses rightly that this relationship must not be characterised as contractual so as to make the claim sound in contract (p. 173). However, it may be that it savours sufficiently of a contract to rebut the defendant's plea that the *lex loci delicti* rather than the law governing their relationship as host driver and guest passenger must be applied.

279. Cavers, p. 175.

280. Cavers, p. 177.

281. Cavers, p. 180; for the notion of "centring" see pp. 183, 188.

282. Cavers, p. 183.

283. Cavers, p. 189.

284. Cavers, p. 194.

285. De Nova, *loc. cit.*, p. 604.

286. The question does not appear to have attracted sufficient attention whether this is always the rule of the *lex validitatis*, or the law which protects a party from his own follies, the law which accords a right to the plaintiff or a defence or counter-claim to the defendant.

287. *Richards* v. *U.S.*, 369 US 1; 7 L.ed. 2d 492 (1962).

287a. See *Neumeier* v. *Kuehner*, 31 N.Y. 2d 128, 133, 286 N.E. 2d 454, 457, 335 N.Y.S. 2d 64, 72 (1972), foreshadowed in *Tooker* v. *Lopez* 24 N.Y. 2d 560, 583, 585; 140 N.E. 2d 394, 403, 404; 301 N.Y.S. 2d 519, 531, 532-33 (1969).

288. See below Nos. 41-43, pp. 63-67.

289. See p. 38.

290. See below Nos. 56-68, pp. 95-98.

291. For a discussion of this view see de Nova, *loc. cit.*, pp. 570-590.

292. Italy, France, Netherlands, Germany, Great Britain, United States.

293. Mann, *Hague Rec.* 132 (1971 I), 107, at pp. 115-121.

294. See Lipstein, [1972 B] *Cambridge L.J.*, 67, at p. 73; Mann, pp. 134-144 and see below, p. 66 and n. 28. But see Frank, *Rabels Z.*, 34 (1970), 56.

295. The practice in other Federal States yields less significant results from the point of view of a general theory of the conflict of laws; see Castel, *Hague Rec.* 126 (1969 I), 1-109.

PART II. THE RELATIONSHIP BETWEEN PUBLIC AND PRIVATE INTERNATIONAL LAW

Section 21. The Influence of Public International Law upon Domestic Private International Law

41. During the last 100 years the question has been raised frequently whether Private International Law is regulated by certain overriding principles of Public International Law.[1] Upon analysis this question resolves itself into two. The first is whether there exist rules of international law bearing upon the conflict of laws; the second is whether such rules, if existing, can exercise any direct influence upon domestic systems of conflict of laws.

The second problem requires some explanation. International Law, being a system of laws governing the relation between States, does not contain any specific rules of private law. Apart from treaty obligations (which may be extensive) in the field of Private International Law[2] States are not bound to introduce any uniform rules of private law, criminal law or any other branch of law, such as Private International Law. International responsibility for denial of justice is not incurred for the mere reason that a country failed to adopt a particular rule or set of rules of domestic law. But there is denial of justice when the fundamental principles of law as observed by all nations are violated. Such are, *inter alia*, the rules: *audi alteram partem*,[3] *nemo judex in propria causa*,[4] *ut res magis valeat quam pereat*,[5] restitution equals reparation,[6] and the prohibition of self-help,[7] but contrary to the belief of some[8] they are not rules bearing upon the substance of domestic law including Private International Law. They may well constitute criteria which Public International Law furnishes in order to assess whether a system of private law of a particular country complies with certain international standards. But Public International Law does not lay down rules of private law proper. However, even if there existed rules of Public International Law which prescribed the adoption of any specific rules of domestic law, including rules of the conflict of laws, such rules could not be self-executing. Failure to comply with what might be called "preliminary" rules of Public International Law would not have any immediate effect in domestic law;[9] in the international sphere it would lead to State responsibility resulting in damages. In the words of Ago: "Il ne s'agirait donc jamais de l'existence de cette norme coutumière internationale concernant directement le droit international privé".[10]

In addition to the principles discussed and dismissed above, the supporters of the internationalist school of Private International Law, in their search for rules of Private Law embodied in Public International Law, have only been able to detect a very limited range of rules, altogether not more than 8 in number.[11] Upon examination, they are either not principles of Public International Law or they are not principles of Private International Law. They are:

(1) Every State must have a system of Private International Law;
(2) States must not exclude the application of foreign law altogether; [12]
(3) States may exclude foreign law on grounds of public policy; [13]
(4) No State may impose its own rules relating to status upon persons who are merely temporary residents;
(5) Immovables are governed by the *lex situs*, and rights in movables acquired in virtue of a previous *lex situs* must be respected;
(6) Form is governed by the *lex loci actus*.[14]
(7) Procedure is governed by the *lex fori*.[14a]
(8) Free choice is allowed for contracts.[14b]

42. Of these eight principles the first four are preliminary or directory rules of Public International Law. They indicate a certain tendency to be followed by States. They do not prescribe the application of any one particular rule of Private International Law, such as whether the law of nationality or of domicile governs status, or which law is to apply to a contract or tort, or whether one legal system is to govern a succession as a whole or whether succession to movables is to be governed by the personal law of the deceased (and, if so, whether this is the law of his nationality or his domicile), while succession to immovables is governed by the lex situs.[15] Instead, the universal acceptance of public policy as a corrective controlling the normal application of foreign law shows that States cannot agree on any general standards of a material or conflictual character.

In fact most countries possess a system of Private International Law and no country refuses categorically to recognise or to apply foreign law altogether. This attitude is not, however, identical with the implementation of a duty prescribed by Public International Law to introduce any particular rule of Private International Law, let alone with adoption of a uniform set of rules of Private International Law.

It merely reflects obedience to the general principles of Public International Law which require the observation of minimum standards of justice and abstention from illegal discrimination.

The last four principles set out above are, it must be admitted, true principles of Private International Law, but they are not rules of Public International Law. In the first place, they are not universally applied [16] and yet no complaint has ever been raised on this ground.[17]

In the second place, even if these principles were applied by all countries in identical circumstances, such a course of action may lead to a uniform practice only. It would not necessarily provide evidence of the existence of principles of International Law to the same effect,[18] although it must be admitted that a new standard of conduct may have crystallised.[19]

However, in the *Boll* Case [20] decided by the International Court of Justice, Judge Sir Hersch Lauterpacht asserted that the principle of public policy had acquired this character and that it is also applicable by an International Court or Tribunal.[21] The latter assertion will be discussed later on where the role of rules of the conflict of laws in international tribunals must be examined.[22] The question remains, in the particular circumstances of that case, whether it was alleged to operate as a part of customary international law or whether it was said to be implied in treaties. As regards the first, whether the principle of public policy is a general principle of law in the meaning of article 38 of the Statute of the Court, the answer must be as follows: In domestic law public policy is a means of excluding foreign law which is normally applicable according to the rules of Private International Law, and of substituting some other system of law, normally the *lexi fori*. However, since domestic law is free to determine whether and in what circumstances it is to be applied in the first instance, the exception of public policy is merely an affirmation in general terms of that freedom to apply foreign or domestic law within the framework of Public International Law, i.e. subject to the minimum standards of justice and without illegal discrimination.[23] Thus the principle of public policy is neither a rule nor a standard forming part of Public International Law. Moreover, it fails to fulfil its function when the International Court of Justice applies its own rules of international conflict of laws. Here public policy, by operating negatively in excluding the law of a state so found to be applicable, fails in its positive function of replacing the rejected domestic law of a foreign State by the *lex fori*. The latter is international law itself, in the eyes of which domestic law is only a fact.[24] Thus public policy in its negative and positive function in an international tribunal administering international law is either identical with customary international law or it expresses the principle that, within its own sphere, a State is sovereign and free unless bound by a treaty.

If it should be argued that public policy as a general principle supplants treaties, the following questions arise: Are all treaties subject to the exception that States may disregard their individual provisions and may substitute for the latter the provisions of their own domestic law when their sensitive areas are affected?[24a] Alternatively, are only those treaties subject to the exception which themselves lay down choice of law rules?[24b] While the answer to the first question must clearly be in the negative, it would seem, as regards the second, that a question of treaty interpretation is involved and not one of customary international law. The modern practice, which insists on the inclusion of a clause reserving the right of States to reject foreign domestic law, which is applicable according to the treaty, if it is "manifestly" against public policy, supports the contention that in the absence of such a clause the reservation of public policy is not necessarily to be implied.[24c]

43. *Legislative Jurisdiction according to Public International Law and Choice of Law Rules.* Recently it has been asserted by an authoritative voice [25] that the distribution of legislative (sometimes called prescriptive) jurisdiction by Public International Law must determine the substance or content of rules of Private International Law.[26] By stressing the importance of legislative jurisdiction and of its control by Public International Law, emphasis is placed upon the power of a State to impose its law on persons and situations at home and abroad. Seen in this light, the process of choice of law is one of self-limitation, not of applying foreign law. This process, it will be remembered,[27] is appropriate to the determination of the range of public law of any one country, seeing that foreign public law is never applied by the *forum* though it may be taken into account as a datum irrespective of whether the *lex fori* or foreign law applies.[28] It is notable that the recent protagonist of the internationalist doctrine of jurisdiction draws his inspiration from criminal law,[29] labour law,[30] tax law,[31] the law of bankruptcy,[32] anti-trust legislation,[33] procedure and jurisdiction [34] and exchange control legislation,[35] all of which are only concerned with the boundaries of their own operation to the exclusion altogether of foreign law bearing this character. In applying the principle of legislative jurisdiction to Private International Law proper, which involves the choice between

local and foreign law, Dr. Mann resuscitates Beale [36] and seeks, once again, to pinpoint the sovereign whose power to exercise legislative jurisdiction according to Public International Law must be respected by Private International Law. Even if the "legally relevant contact" is made the criterion, as Dr. Mann suggests,[37] the result is not more encouraging than it was to Beale's successors in the United States.[38] Torts are said by Public International Law to fall within the legislative jurisdiction of the *locus delicti* because of the admonitory character of the law of tort.[39] However, this leaves all the well-known problems wide open: where is the *locus delicti* in interstate torts; what is the effect of rules sounding in tort which are compensatory?

Title to property is said to be governed by the *lex situs*, but as was pointed out above,[40] this principle is not universally applied, especially where general assignments on marriage, death or bankruptcy are concerned, and Dr. Mann must allow here an exception in favour of the personal law.[41]

These discrepancies between theory and practice lay the Neo-Bealians open to the same charge as that which was raised against Beale himself. If vague generalities cannot serve the purpose, only *a priori* rules satisfy an overriding doctrine of legislative jurisdiction which seeks to determine when domestic and when foreign law is to be applied in order to solve questions of choice of private law. It is quite another matter when the spatial operation of public law (criminal, labour, tax, anti-trust, procedure) must be determined. Here the need to delimit the actual operation of such laws may well be served best by reliance on the division of legislative competence of States according to Public International Law as a yardstick.[42]

Section 22. Private International Law as Part of Public International Law—Choice of Law before International Tribunals

44. It has been shown above that Public International Law does not contain any specific rules bearing on Private International Law. It is quite another question whether Private International Law has a role to play in Public International Law. If an international dispute arises involving State responsibility for damage to the proprietary interests in the broadest sense, whether they be contractual or are represented by title to property, movable or immovable, alleged to be vested in an alien or in a foreign State, an international tribunal must ascertain, first of all, whether a right of a proprietary nature in the sense

described above is vested in the alien or in the foreign State concerned. This question must be determined before it is possible to turn to the principal problem, which is whether in the light of Public International Law a right of a proprietary nature has been infringed so as to constitute an international wrong.[43] For this purpose the International Tribunal must exercise a choice of law in accordance with a set of rules of Private International Law. The problem is only which system of Private International Law is to supply these rules. In response to this need the practice of international tribunals over the last century has developed independent rules of Private International Law which may be called "Rules of International Conflict of Laws".[44] These rules cover a broad range of situations and do not appear to differ much from domestic rules of Private International Law, were it not for some overriding special characteristics. In the first place, international tribunals do not possess a *lex fori* in matters of private law. The *lex fori* of international tribunals consists of Public International Law as developed by custom and treaties. The American-Venezuelan Commission said in *William*'s Case: [45]

> "it is a well-settled principle in common law jurisdictions, and a recognised one in civil law countries, that obligations are to be enforced according to the *lex fori* which here is the treaty and the public law".

Thus, while Private International Law within a State may choose between the application of the municipal law of the court concerned and of foreign law as an alternative source, international courts, owing to the absence of a *lex fori* in matters of private law, must elect between two or more systems of municipal law, none of which can claim the privileged position of *lex curiae*.[46]

It follows, in the second place, that the doctrine of *renvoi* cannot apply. If an international system of conflict of laws accepted a reference back to the *lex fori* it would defeat its own ends, seeing that the reference back would lead to the application, not of municipal, but of international law. It is therefore not surprising that not a single case involving *renvoi* can be found among the great number of international decisions.

On the other hand, it is conceivable that an international tribunal, having ascertained with the help of its own international rules of the conflict of laws that a certain system of municipal law applies, adopts this system as a whole, including its rules of municipal private international law. These rules may refer to yet another system of municipal law by a process known as transmission or *Weiterverweisung*.[47] Such a situation should not be allowed to arise in international courts. It would mean that an international tribunal identifies itself with the courts of a particular country, so as to adopt the law of that country as the *lex curiae*, before embarking upon a final choice of law. This would amount to a capitulation of the international court before the Private International Law of a particular country. A reference by international rules of the conflict of laws to some system of municipal law must be final.

In the third place, it follows that in a system of international conflict of laws the principle of public policy must fulfil a different function than in municipal private international law. Within the latter system, the principle of public policy operates so as to substitute the municipal law of the *lex fori* for the system of foreign law ordinarily applicable. Seeing that the *lex fori* of international tribunals consists of international law alone, the function of public policy in an international system of conflict of laws can be only to exclude the operation of foreign private law. It is incapable of substituting another system of private law. Consequently, international public policy can only deny a property right, the violation of which forms the subject of an international reclamation. It can never allow a property right where the foreign law, ordinarily applicable, has denied its existence. It must be admitted that this contention is not borne out by the practice of the Permanent Court of International Justice. In the *Serbian and Brazilian Loan* Cases,[48] it was held that an international court, when applying the municipal law of a particular country, must seek to apply it as it would be applied by that country, including its principles of public policy.

However, if an international court, with the help of its own international rules of conflict of laws, finds that a particular system of municipal law applies, it cannot serve any useful purpose to apply also the rules of public policy of that system which are directed against the application of yet another system of municipal law.[49] But it must be admitted that the answer would have to be different, if the principle of transmission or *Weiterverweisung*, which was rejected above, were to be accepted.

Generally speaking, the practice of international tribunals has not developed on the lines followed by the Permanent Court of International Justice. The case of *The Enterprize* decided by the Anglo-American Claims Commission,[50] represents a strong precedent in favour of our proposition that the principles of public policy, for the purposes of international courts, are furnished by international law. The facts were as follows. In 1835, an American vessel carrying slaves belonging to American owners took refuge in Bermuda, owing to stress of weather. The Court of Bermuda ordered the slaves to be freed pursuant to the Act of 3 and 4 Wm. IV c. 73 (1833) abolishing slavery in Great Britain and her dependencies. In the course of the claim for damages against Great Britain, the tribunal had to decide whether the court of Bermuda was entitled to apply the English statute in respect of *res in transitu* on board a vessel and which were ordinarily subject to American law as their former *lex rei sitae,* or as the law of the flag. It was clear that the Bermudan Court had applied the English statute on grounds of public policy. The question was therefore whether the principles of public policy to be considered by the international tribunal were those of the law of Bermuda which rejected slavery or of the *lex fori*, i.e., international law, which at that time did not. The Commission, including, it would appear, Hornby, the British Commissioner, who delivered a dissenting judgment,[51] decided that the principles of public policy were prescribed by international law and, by a majority, allowed the claim. Bates, the Umpire said: [52]

> "It was well known that slavery had been conditionally abolished in nearly all the British Dominions about six months before . . . No one can deny that slavery is contrary to the principles of justice and humanity and can only be established in any country by law. At the time of the transaction on which the claim is founded, slavery existed by law in several countries and was not wholly abolished in the British Dominions. It could not, then, be contrary to the law of nations, and *The Enterprize* was as much entitled to protection as though her cargo consisted of any other description of property. The conduct of the authorities of Bermuda was a violation of the law of nations . . ."

The remarks of Upham, the American Commissioner, are even more forceful, but it is submitted that they are too sweeping. He said: [53]

> "There is but one ground on which it can be contended that the Act of 3 and 4 Wm. IV c. 73 overrules the principles that I have laid down [i.e., that the law of the port may not be applied to foreign vessels in port and to property on board] and that is that the municipal law of England is paramount to the absolute rights of other governments when they come in conflict with each other.

Such a position virtually abolishes the entire code of international law. If one state can at pleasure revoke such a law, any other state may do the same thing, and the whole system of international intercourse becomes a mere matter of arbitrary will and of universal violence."

It may be useful to refer to a few more awards. In the case of *The Maria Luz*,[54] the Peruvian Government claimed damages from Japan on the ground that Japanese Courts had acted illegally in disallowing the claim of a Peruvian Captain for the restoration of escaped Chinese coolies who were under a contract to him. The arbitrator said:

"We have arrived at the conviction . . . that the Japanese Government acted in good faith, in virtue of its own laws and customs, without infringing the general prescriptions of the law of nations or the stipulations of particular treaties."

Another example is furnished by the decision of the tribunal in *Reparation Commission* v. *U.S.A.*[55] The facts were as follows. Shortly before the outbreak of war between the U.S.A. and Germany in 1917, the Standard Oil Co. sold its shares in a German Company to a German national in consideration of a sum the payment of which was deferred, supplemented by a deposit of securities as a guarantee. The securities were subsequently seized by the American Custodian of Enemy Property. The claim before the tribunal involved the question whether the contract of sale was valid and whether the American Company had acquired a lien over the securities. The Tribunal said:

"Whereas the . . . securities . . . were seized as enemy property by the Enemy Property Custodian, the latter, when opposition was lodged by the Standard Oil Co., asserted his belief in the good faith of the sale, but none the less by a decision . . . declared it to be null and void. Whereas this decision, being prompted only by reasons of public order, could not lead the Tribunal to consider the sale as null . . ."

In the fourth place, the absence of a *lex fori* in matters of private law explains why only a comparatively small number of cases involved difficulties of what is generally known as conflicts of characterisation. Such conflicts, it may be remembered, are not infrequent in municipal private international law. They may arise when a Court must interpret the meaning of a legal concept contained in a rule of private or of private international law. These terms may have one meaning according to the *lex fori* and another according to the law ordinarily applicable. The tribunals, the practice of which is under review today, have not followed any consistent line in matters of characterisation. In general they characterised according to the law of one of the countries which were parties to the dispute.[56] But it is impossible to ascertain the reasons why the characterisation according to one system of laws was chosen in preference to any other. Sometimes it cannot even be stated according to which system of laws the tribunals characterised.[57]

In the fifth place the method of proving foreign municipal law in international courts must be noted. The Permanent Court of International Justice held in the *Serbian and Brazilian Loan* Cases: [58]

> "Though bound to apply municipal law when circumstances so require, the Court, which is a tribunal of international law and which, in this capacity, is deemed itself to know what this law is, is not obliged also to know the municipal law of the various countries. All that can be said in this respect is that the Court may possibly be obliged to obtain knowledge regarding the municipal law which has to be applied. And this it must do, either by means of evidence furnished it by the parties, or by means of any researches which the Court may think fit to undertake or to cause to be undertaken."

And again:

> "For the Court itself to undertake its own construction of municipal law, leaving on one side existing judicial decisions, with the ensuing danger of contradicting the construction which has been placed on such law by the highest national tribunal and which, in its results, seems to the Court reasonable, would not be in conformity with the task for which the Court has been established . . ." [59]

The Court based its conclusions with respect to French law on citations of publicists and judicial decisions of French Courts.[60] The same approach was chosen by the great majority of international tribunals,[61] although in some cases emphasis was laid upon the opinion of experts,[62] and in others upon the practice of municipal courts.[63] In the *Hudson Bay Co.* Claim [64] and in the *Puget Sound Agricultural Co.* Claim,[65] which involved disputes over titles to land not yet under the sovereignty of any State, the tribunal applied the principles of natural justice.

Finally, nationality is of paramount importance, for unlike municipal courts, international tribunals must consider not only whether a right exists and according to which system of law, but they must also determine whether the plaintiff and his claim are so intimately connected with one of the States subject to the jurisdiction of the tribunal as to confer upon it the necessary competence to adjudicate.

45. If the preliminary investigation establishes the existence of a property right under domestic law and that the right has been violated by the defendant State in breach of Public International Law involving State responsibility, a defence based on a domestic statute of limitations,[66] a domestic rule that *actio personalis moritur cum persona* [67] or a domestic rule that the State is not liable for the acts of its officials [68] is of no avail.

> "The right of a person to sue a Government under domestic law is not conclusive with respect to rights that may be invoked in behalf of such a person under international law." [69]

The same applies to the measure of damages, the rate of exchange and the question of interest.[70]

The preliminary investigation is only concerned with the existence of property rights under municipal law. The question whether a violation of the right thus ascertained is actionable must be decided, for the purposes of an international reclamation before an international tribunal, according to the principles of international law. The Rules of International Conflict of Laws cover a fairly wide range of situations including proof of foreign law,[71] corporations [72] and partnerships,[73] contracts and quasi-contracts,[74] torts,[75] property [76] and successions.[77]

Even if the content of these rules of International Conflict of Laws appear more often than not to be the same as those of domestic Private International Law, the special characteristics set out above (para. 44) are so strong as to exclude any identity of these two systems of Private International Law. For the same reason there exists no hierarchy, in the conflict of laws, of a supreme international and subordinate municipal systems of Private International Law.

At the same time the existence of Rules of International Conflict of Laws, much neglected hitherto, eliminates the need to make provision in international agreement of a private law nature between States or between a State or an individual for the application of "general principles of law" observed by all nations.[78] If it is the purpose of this device to eliminate any difficulties arising out of the absence of any particular system of domestic Private International Law which can determine the law applicable to the preliminary question as to whether a right of a proprietary nature exists, the answer must be that the Rules of International Conflict of Laws, which were outlined above, are sufficiently developed to dispose of these difficulties. If this device is used because the parties are unwilling to allow any one legal system to apply which is connected with the transaction and seek to exclude the application of specific domestic law altogether,[79] it must be asked whether the parties can do so effectively. In an international tribunal the rules of international conflict of laws, in domestic courts the rules of domestic Private International Law continue to apply and may perhaps override the choice of general principles of law.[80]

Section 23. Recognition and the Application of Foreign Law [81]

46. It is necessary to draw attention at this stage to the principle, alleged to have been developed in English and American Law, which has been summed up as follows some 25 years ago:

> "Recognition, being retroactive and dating back to the moment at which the newly recognised Government established itself in power, its effect is to preclude the courts of law of the recognising State from questioning the legality or validity of the acts, both legislative and executive, past and future, of that Government." [82]

This principle is known in England as the rule in *Luther* v. *Sagor* [83] and in the United States as the "Act of State" doctrine represented most recently by the *Sabbatino* Case,[84] preceded by many other decisions to the same effect. It is less rigidly applied or even unknown in other countries.[85] Read literally, it only prohibits courts from "questioning the legality or validity of legislative and administrative acts". If this interpretation is followed, the rule is restricted to the prohibition to allow an action in tort in England or the United States on the strength of an allegation that a foreign legislative or administrative act is illegal under the foreign law concerned, but does not oblige the *lex fori* to apply the foreign law concerned or to give effect to the foreign administrative act. Unfortunately the development has gone far beyond this point, due perhaps to the fact that in common law countries actions, which in civil law countries enforce title to goods by a *rei vindicatio*,[86] are framed in tort even if directed against a third party. Thus the prohibition to institute an action in tort as a result of legislation or of an administrative act by a recognised government has a much more far reaching effect. Conceived as a barrier to prevent individuals with a grievance against a foreign government from by-passing the normal channels, i.e., from proceeding against that government in its own courts in respect of acts of a public law nature, or from pressing claims based on a violation of international law in respect of aliens,[87] the principle may have its origin [88] in the English doctrine of acts of State, which prohibits actions in tort brought in England by aliens in respect of acts abroad by individuals whose acts are authorised or ratified by the Government in the United Kingdom.[89] As it appears today in the books, it may not stand up to scrutiny [90] and will perhaps assume finally its proper role, which has now become two-fold. This role is, firstly, to preclude a claim for damages in tort against an individual for a violation of foreign Public or Public International Law committed by a Government and, secondly, to determine which of two competing sets of rules enacted or which measures taken by rival authorities in the same country are to be regarded as the law and the acts of the Government of that country, but no more. Thus understood the principle does contain a choice of law rule; it concerns the proof of foreign law and the exclusion of Public International Law as a basis of an action in tort, in disregard of foreign law which is normally applicable, against persons who carried out the act or who acquired property in consequence of the act. It is believed that this is the proper function and meaning of the rule.

47. In England and in the countries which look to the common law of England, the judgment of the Court of Appeal in *Luther* v. *Sagor* [91] gave the lead; but it was a case *primae impressionis* and its interpretation depends much on the stress which is laid upon the respective arguments adduced by the three Lords Justices who decided it.[92] If authority is to be sought for this decision, it is to be found in three judgments of the Supreme Court of the United States on which the English Court of Appeal relied.

Of these *Williams* v. *Bruffy* [93] established a purely negative rule. *If the ordinary principles of the conflict of laws refer to the law of a particular foreign country*, the enactments of insurrectionist authorities may be disregarded, if these authorities were never recognised and did not survive.[94] *Underhill* v. *Hernandez* [95] established a positive and a negative rule. *If the ordinary principles of the conflict of laws refer to the law of a particular foreign country*, the enactments and acts of revolutionary authorities are treated retroactively as the law of the foreign country and as the executive acts of a foreign government, once these revolutionary authorities have been recognised as the government by the executive of the forum. In a conflict of laws in time, the rules and acts of the government which was recognised last prevails. The fact that prior to recognition the measures were illegal acts of individual rebels is irrelevant. Furthermore the question whether an act, lawful by the *lex loci*, constitutes a breach of Public International Law can only be considered by governments and by international tribunals.

Oetjen v. *Central Leather Co.*[96] enlarges upon the principle established in *Underhill* v. *Hernandez.*[97] *If the ordinary principles of the conflict of laws refer to the law of a particular foreign country,*[98] the government of which has been recognised by the executive of the forum, the enactments and acts of that government cannot be examined by the courts of the forum for the purpose of determining whether damages are to be awarded against an individual on the ground of a breach of international law. The much discussed decision of the Supreme Court of the United States in *Banco Nacional de Cuba* v. *Sabbatino,*[99] has added little, but its existence has been the first reason for its erosion by the Hickenlooper Amendment attached to the Foreign Assistance Act, 1964, enacted in the United States.[100]

48. It is now necessary to consider the rule, as commonly understood, its limits and its justification at the present time.

In the first place, recognition is not the factor which determines whether foreign law is to be applied by the courts of the forum.[101] Otherwise the laws of all recognised governments could claim respect. It is the task of the rules of Private International Law of the forum to determine this conflict. Recognition determines only which of two competing sets of regulations within one country must be regarded as the law of the foreign country, once the Private International Law of the forum has referred to the law of the particular foreign country.[102]

At the same time recognition of a government confers upon the acts and measures of the recognised authority the character of an act by a public authority and attributes to it the character of a datum, which has to be taken into account by the courts of the forum whenever the operation of foreign public law must be considered.

In the second place, the rule does not apply to the decisions of foreign courts. Here again recognition determines only whether the courts established by the predecessor government or the bodies set up by the new government are courts, the pronouncements of which can be recognised and enforced by the forum, *if* the courts of the foreign country have jurisdiction according to the law of the court of the recognising country.[103]

In the third place, despite the past and present trend to the contrary in common law countries,[104] it would seem that the regulations of foreign bodies which have not been recognised can nevertheless be applied in accordance with the rules of Private International Law of the forum, if they are in fact enforced in the foreign country concerned.[105] Recognition by the government of the forum is the best evidence for determining whether the regulations and measures of foreign bodies are to be regarded as the law of the foreign country and the acts of public authorities, but it is not conclusive evidence.

In the fourth place, recognition does not bind the courts of the recognising State unconditionally to respect the law of the recognised State, if the rules of Private International Law of the forum refer to that law, or to accept the effects, in private law, of the acts of the executive organs of the recognised government. The existence of the latter cannot be denied, and they constitute a datum or data,[106] but no more. This latter aspect must be developed in some detail.

Section 24. Scrutiny of, and Refusal to Apply or to Respect, the Law and the Executive Acts of a Foreign Recognised Government

49. The contention that the rule known as the act of State principle or the rule in *Luther* v. *Sagor* [107] is concerned, at least in part, with proof of foreign law when the court is confronted by two conflicting sets of rules enacted by rival authorities in a State, is borne out by the practice and literature on the scrutiny of the constitutional validity of foreign law.[108] On a lower level the same problem is posed, if the rule of foreign law is to be found in delegated legislation and it is alleged that such legislation contravenes an Enabling Act of the *lex causae*. Again, it may be alleged that a treaty entered into by the State of the *lex causae*, has not been incorporated into the law of the State which is applicable, although the Constitution of that State so requires, if the treaty is to be effective. Conversely it may be argued that, according to the constitutional law of the foreign *lex causae*, a previous treaty has been superseded by subsequent domestic legislation. Finally, the question may present itself in two stages, if it is contended, firstly, that the applicable rule of foreign law violates a precept of public international

law and, secondly, that the constitution of the foreign State concerned invalidates all provisions of its domestic law which are contrary to the principles of Public International Law accepted by that State.[109]

If the foreign law concerned permits the judicial control of the constitutional validity of its statutes, the forum may also exercise this control, unless the foreign law concerned reserves for a special court [110] the determination, with binding effect *erga omnes*, whether a particular rule violates the constitution and is invalid.

Thus, in all these circumstances, the rule of foreign law applicable in the circumstances, may be disregarded and the foreign executive act can be treated as invalid because the forum may determine the constitutional validity according to the *lex causae*. This conclusion does not, however, lead necessarily to another, namely that an action in tort may be brought in the forum against a member of the foreign government or a third party who has acquired property on the strength of the foreign law or of the foreign executive act. The answer to the latter question must depend upon whether the executive measure simply ceases to be a datum or must henceforth be treated as an illegal act.

50. Those who believe that the foreign act of State doctrine is a precept of Public International Law [111] seek to mitigate its effects by asserting that a breach of Public International Law by the foreign government concerned either deprives the act of its validity altogether, or at least relieves the courts in other countries from giving effect to it.[112] The conclusion that a foreign government has committed a breach of Public International Law and that the foreign executive measure can be disregarded as void involves the appreciation and determination of extraneous factors and the application of a system of law which is not, properly speaking, that of the forum. It is, therefore, not surprising that this result has only been reached rarely.[113] It must be stressed, however, once more that the problem cannot be disposed of by the argument that laws or executive measures are void if they conflict with Public International Law.[114] Whether domestic law is void can only be determined by reference to the constitutional law of the foreign country concerned; as shown above, this scrutiny is only possible during the process of proving foreign law and only if the foreign law concerned permits generally the judicial review of the constitutionality of its legislation.[115] In the absence of such a finding by a competent court, the act remains at least a datum. Any principle of the foreign law postulating the primacy of International Law is thus safeguarded.

51. It is another matter whether the forum will give effect to foreign law, which is applicable according to its rules of Private International Law, or to foreign executive measures, if they infringe Public International Law. Since the choice and application of foreign law is in the discretion of the *lex fori* and since the foreign act of State doctrine is equally a doctrine of domestic law, it is clear that the forum need not apply foreign law or give effect to foreign acts, if they offend manifestly against the public policy of the forum. The problem is, therefore, whether a breach of Public International Law as such offends against the public policy of the forum or whether it is only a factor to be taken into account in deciding whether foreign law which is normally applicable is to be applied in the particular case, or whether a foreign executive act is to be recognised and given effect.

The answer is easy, if the foreign law or the foreign executive measure in issue runs counter to a fundamental principle of the *lex fori* as embodied in the Constitution of the latter [116] and, especially if the local Constitution sanctions the primacy of Public International Law. In all other circumstances it would appear that, when confronted with a plea that the foreign law or the foreign executive act offends against Public International Law, courts in a variety of countries have considered the rules of Public International Law incidentally only as a facet of a broader notion of local public policy.[117] This attitude is to be approved since, in the absence of the principle of primacy of Public International Law in the *lex causae* or the *lex fori*, the substance of the individual rule of foreign law or of the particular executive act and not the formal violation of a rule of Public International Law must determine whether the rule or act offends against the basic social, political and moral foundations of the *lex fori*. At the same time, reliance on the negative function of public policy rather than on negative reaction to a breach of International Law makes it possible to deny effect to the foreign law or foreign executive measure in issue irrespective of whether the person affected is an alien, a stateless person or a national of the country of the *lex causae*. Thus the foreign law or the foreign measure is accorded or denied effect uniformly and without discrimination in accordance with the general standards of the *lex fori*. Only in the United States rigid adherence to the foreign act of State doctrine has made this course impracticable.[118]

Section 25. Conclusions

52. The result of the foregoing examination can be summed up thus: Private International Law as part of the law of individual countries is domestic law, unfettered by special rules of Public International Law and unrelated to the rules of International Conflict of Laws. Subject only to the general standards of Public International Law, it is determined by the policies, traditions and standards of justice of the individual countries, and free from controls except in Federal states, where the Constitution may impose curbs. Students of the conflict of laws have not been content, however, with this insight. Instead, attempts have been made again and again to determine the philosophical background of these rules. Apparently, the knowledge that they are technical rules which (in most instances) [119] have no substantive content of their own and only point to some legal system as being applicable was felt to be insufficient. There is some justification for such discontent, for a crucial question has remained unsolved: In the absence of a specific rule of Private International Law, is the court to develop a new rule by way of analogy or otherwise, or is it to apply its own *lex fori* on the ground that in the particular circumstance there is no reference to foreign law?

The various attempts to find a fundamental approach which have been made in recent years have been surveyed elsewhere.[120] As an instrument of internationalisation,[121] reconciling conflicting interests, rational co-ordination or, generally to promote justice,[122] it does not appear to represent principles or to serve purposes which are not common to every legal system as a whole. It may be suggested here that the basic problem is whether the operation of laws is limited *ratione loci* and *ratione personae* or whether, in the absence of any specific restriction, laws purport to operate outside the jurisdiction. It is clear that neither the *lex fori* nor foreign law can claim to be applied elsewhere. The former is incapable of exporting itself on its own and the latter cannot be imported into the forum except by a precept of the *lex fori* embodied in a rule of its Private International Law. The problem is, therefore, to determine the range of the *lex fori* by examining the relationship between the *lex fori* and foreign law.

If the *lex fori* is a closed and self-sufficient system, it follows that the *lex fori* applies even to situations containing a foreign element which form the object of litigation in the forum [123] unless a specific rule of Private International Law of the forum *restricts* the operation of the *lex fori* and, at the same time, *introduces* foreign law as an exception.[124]

If the *lex fori* is primarily restricted to situations having a connection with the country of the *forum* on personal or territorial grounds, it follows that a broad range of rules of Private International Law must determine which foreign law is applicable. Otherwise no legal system might be applicable, or only the *lex fori*, thus restoring the closed and universal character of the *lex fori*.

It is probably difficult to state with certainty which legal system in the world follows either view. Some indications are provided by the rules of Private International Law themselves, whether they are rudimentary or detailed, whether they are expressed in terms of the ordinary conflict rules [125] or of spatially conditioned internal rules,[126] and whether *renvoi* is accepted or not.[127] The analysis of the practice and the literature in the United States [128] point to the assertion of closed and self-sufficient systems; an examination of the recent practice in England points in the opposite direction [129] in accordance with what appears to be a European trend. The development and refinement of orthodox rules of Private International Law [130] or alternatively an increased emphasis on spatially conditional internal rules [130] will follow from adherence respectively to the former or the latter trend. Given what is believed to be the trend in Europe to deny a universalistic character to each legal system, the American experience, based on a contrary trend, is not likely to assist greatly.

NOTES TO PART II

1. For an account of the problem up to the Second World War see Lipstein (1942), 27 *Transactions of the Grotius Society*, 142, at pp. 142-149 with lit. notes 1-4 and see Maury, *Hague Rec.* 57 (1936 III), 329 at 356; Makarov in *Mélanges Streit* (1939), 535; Balogh, *ibid.*, p. 71; Niederer in *Schweizerisches Jahrbuch für Internationales Recht*, 5 (1948), p. 63; *Einführung in das internationale Privatrecht* (2 ed. 1956), pp. 102-114; Stevenson (1952), 52 *Col.L.R.*, 561; Maridakis, *Ius et Lex, Festgabe für Gutzwiller* (1959), 253; Wortley, *Hague Rec.* 85 (1954 I), 245; Riphagen, *ibid.*, 102 (1961 I), 219; Hambro, *Varia Juris Gentium, Liber Amicorum François* (1959), 132, *Hague Rec.* 105 (1962 I), 1; Makarov in Strupp-Schlochauer, *Wörterbuch des Völkerrechts*, II (1961), 129-133; Schnitzer in *Mélanges Guggenheim* (1968), p. 102; Rigaux, *Revista española de derecho internacional*, 21 (1968), 720; Batiffol, *ibid.*, 25 (1972), 77; Pocar, *Italian Yearbook of International Law*, (1975), 179; Schnitzer, *Z.f.RV.* 17, (1976), 13, 19; Neuhaus, *German Yearbook of International Law*, 21 (1978), 60.

2. Attention must be drawn to the great number of treaties concluded by the Hague Conferences on Private International Law (see for the treaties in force, as regards those conducted before 1914 Gutzwiller, *Schweizerisches Jahrbuch für Internationales Recht*, 2 (1945), pp. 48-99; Kegel, *Internationales Privatrecht* (3 ed.

1971), pp. 87 ff.; for the period after 1945 see *ibid.*, pp. 87-90; *Rev.crit.*, 1971, 153-157; Conférence de La Haye, *Recueil des Conventions de La Haye*); by the Socialist States of Eastern Europe: Drobnig, *Osteur. R.* (1960), 154; Uschakow, *ibid.*, 7 (1961), 161; Makarov, *ibid.*, (1969) 1; by the Benelux countries: Rigaux, *Clunet* 1969, 334; *Rev.crit.* 1968, 812; de Winter, *ibid.*, 597. Scandinavian Treaties: see Philip, *Hague Rec.* 96 (1959 I), 245. South and Central American States: Vitta, *Hague Rec.* 126 (1969 I), at pp. 128-133; Makarov, *Quellen des internationalen Privatrechts* (1960 II), Nos. 1-5.

3. Wortley, *loc. cit.*, p. 318; Hambro, *Hague Rec.*, *loc. cit.*, p. 12, citing Ago, *Hague Rec.* 58 (1936 IV), 289-290.

4. Wortley, *loc. cit.*, p. 316.

5. Hambro, *loc. cit.*, p. 12.

6. Wortley, *loc. cit.*, p. 319.

7. Wortley, *loc. cit.*, p. 320.

8. See above note 3.

9. Lipstein, *loc. cit.*, p. 143, n. 3.

10. *Hague Rec.* 58 (1936 IV), p. 291, n. 1.

11. Lipstein, *loc. cit.*, p. 146 and note 25 with lit. to which should be added: von Bar, *Theorie und Praxis des international Privatrechts*, I (2 ed. 1889), paras. 2-5; Pillet, *Principes de droit international privé* (1903), p. 55; *Traité pratique*, I (1923), pp. 18-21; Murad Ferid, *Vom Deutschen zum Europäischen Recht, Festschrift für Doelle* (1963), II, 119 at pp. 127-129.

12. Kahn, *Abhandlungen zum international Privatrecht*, I (1928), 286; see now the observations of Mann, *Hague Rec.* 111 (1964 I), at p. 56, n. 12.

13. *Boll Case (Netherlands* v. *Sweden), I.C.J. Reports 1958*, p. 52; Lipstein (1959), 8 *International and Comparative Law Quarterly*, 506, at p. 520; Batiffol and Francescakis, *Rev.crit.d.c.p.* 1959, p. 259; von Overbeck, in *Ius et Lex, Festgabe für Gutzwiller* (1959), 325; Makarov, *ibid.*, p. 303; Kollewijn, *Nederlands Tijdschrift voor international Recht* 1959, 311 = *Diritto Internazionale*, 14 (1960), 103; M. Weser, *Riv.dir.int.* 1959, 426.

14. See Mann, above, note 12; P. Klein, *Archiv für bürgerliches Recht*, 29 (1906), 102.

14a. Niederer, *Einführung in die allgemeinen Lehren des Internationalen Privatrechts* (3ed. 1961), 107.

14b. Niederer, *ibid.*

15. See Lipstein (1942), 27 *Transactions of the Grotius Society*, 143, at p. 147 with lit. at n. 26.

16. According to Art. 23 of the Introductory Law to the Italian Civil Code of 1942, succession to movables and to immovables is governed by the *lex patriae*. In England, before the Wills Act 1861, the formalities of wills of personalty generally and, after 1861, the formalities of wills of personalty made by aliens were governed, until 1963, by the law of the last domicile of the deceased. In Anglo-American law, the concept of procedure is much broader than in civil law countries and includes limitation of actions, set-off and certain requirements which are *jus cogens*.

17. See the lit. cited by Lipstein (1942), 27 *Transactions of the Grotius Society*, 142, at p. 143, n. 4, especially Bruns, *Fontes Juris Gentium*, ser. B sectio I, tomus I, pp. 454-455; Nussbaum (1942), 42 *Col.L.R.*, 189.

British-Syrian Exchange of Notes, 1 November 1946, *Rev. crit. d.i.p.* 1949, 377; *United Kingdom Treaty Series* No. 37 (1947), Cmd 7140.

18. Lipstein, *loc. cit.*, p. 147 with lit. n. 27.

19. Hambro, *loc. cit.* (above p. 63, n. 1); for a series of theories on the relationship between Public and Private International Law which bear no relation to any

actual practice see Lipstein, *loc. cit.*, p. 148, and notes 28-30 with lit.; de Nova, *Hague Rec.* 118 (1966 II), 438, at pp. 473-477 with lit.; Mann, *Hague Rec.* 111 (1964 I), at p. 22, n. 37.

20. Above, p. 64, n. 13.

21. *I.C.J. Reports 1958*, p. 52, at pp. 79 ff., esp. pp. 89 ff.

22. Below, sec. 22, Nos. 44-45, pp. 67-74.

23. See Lipstein (1959), 8 *International and Comparative Law Quarterly*, 506, at pp. 520-521.

24. Lipstein, *Transactions of the Grotius Society*, 27 (1942), pp. 149, 156-157, and note 67 with references; 29 (1944), pp. 63-66; see also Niboyet, *Traité*, III (1944), No. 1041, p. 562; Batiffol, *Traité élémentaire* (5 ed. 1970), No. 362, p. 431; Schnitzer, *Handbuch des Internationalen Privatrechts* (4 ed. 1950), I, p. 228.

24a. See BGHZ 59, 83; Bleckmann, *ZaöRV* 34 (1974) 112; Schreuer (1978) 27 *International and Comparative Law Quarterly* 1, 3.

24b. See also Kahn-Freund, *Hague Rec.* (1974 III), (195-196).

24c. See Neuhaus, *German Yearbook of International Law* (above p. 63, n. 1) at p. 61 n. 4, who neglects the two aspects stressed here.

25. Mann, *Hague Rec.* 111 (1964 I), pp. 1-162.

26. See also above, p. 29.

27. See also above, pp. 45-46, but see Frank, *Rabels Z.*, 34 (1970) 56.

28. See, e.g., *Re Bettinson's Question*, [1956] Ch. 67; *Regazzoni* v. *Sethia*, [1958] A.C. 301 and *Ralli Bros.* v. *Cia Naviera Sota y Aznar*, [1920] 2 K.B. 287 as interpreted by Mann (1937), 18 *B.Y.I.L.*, 97; *The Halley*, (1868) L.R., 2 P.C. 192, 202 and the cases cited by Lipstein in *Ius Privatum Gentium*, I (1969), 411, at 420-422; cp. Mann, 132; *Hague Rec.* 132 (1971 I), 109 at 189, but see p. 193, n. 47.

29. Mann, *loc. cit.*, at p. 29, n. 30, p. 33; *The Lotus*, *P.C.I.J.*, *Ser. A*, *No. 10 (1927)*, at pp. 36, 39, 47, n. 90; *Reg.* v. *Jameson*, [1896] 2 Q.B. 425, 430; pp. 82 ff.

30. At p. 47, n. 90: *Lauritzen* v. *Larsen*, 345 US 571, 578 (1953).

31. At p. 29, n. 29: *Amsterdam* v. *Min. of Finance* (Israel), International Law Reports 1952, 229, 231; p. 37; p. 48 n. 92: *Trustees & Executors Agency Co.* v. *Federal Commissioner of Taxation* (1933), 49 C.L.R. 220, 325, 239; see also Mann, pp. 109-119.

32. At p. 29, n. 28: *Ex p. Blain* (1879), 12 Ch.D. 522, 528.

33. At pp. 95-108 with cases.

34. At pp. 73 ff.

35. At pp. 122-126.

36. See above, p. 26.

37. At pp. 44, 49, 50; see also pp. 19, 21, 9, but see the curious case posited at pp. 39-40. The criterion seems to have been inspired by the practice of the American Supreme Court set out above, sec. 16.

38. See above, Nos. 25-27, pp. 27-28.

39. At p. 57, but see p. 37.

40. See above, p. 65, n. 16.

41. *Loc. cit.*, at p. 62.

42. Contra Mann, *loc. cit.*, pp. 71-72, but see *passim*, esp. pp. 63-71 and *Hague Rec.* 132 (1971 I), 109-196. It is another matter whether enforcement orders may be made which purport to affect conduct in another country; Mann, *loc. cit.*, p. 97, pp. 127 ff., esp. pp. 145 ff.

43. See *Illinois Central Railroad Case*, Opinions of Commissioners under the Convention concluded September 8, 1923, between the United States and Mexico, I, p. 15 at pp. 17 ff., cited as *Opinions*, I, II, III (3 vols., 1924, 1929, 1931); see

also Feller, *Mexican Claims Commission* (1935), p. 173; De Beus, *The Jurisprudence of the General Claims Commission, United States* v. *Mexico* (1938), pp. 15-21; Ralston, *The Law and Procedure of International Tribunals* (1926), p. 75; *Mexican Union Railways Claim*, Decisions and Opinions of the Commissioners in accordance with the Convention of November 19, 1926, between Great Britain and the United Mexican States (2 vols., 1931, 1933), I, p. 157, at p. 162, henceforth cited as *Decisions*, I, II; *Hoachozo Palestine Land and Development Co. Case*, American-Turkish Claims Settlement under the Agreement of December 24, 1923 (ed. Nielsen, 1937), cited as *American-Turkish Claims*, p. 254, at pp. 259, 260; *Nicholas Marmaras Claim, ibid.*, p. 473, at pp. 479, 480; *Cook* Case (No. 1), *Opinions*, I, p. 318, at p. 321; *Nielsen*, p. 196, at pp. 198-199; *Cook* Case (No. 2), *Opinions*, II, p. 266, at p. 269; Nielsen, *International Law applied to Reclamations* (1933), henceforth cited as Nielsen, p. 389, at pp. 390-391, 395-396; *Ina Hoffman and Dulcie Steinhardt*, American-Turkish Claims, p. 286, at pp. 287-288; see also *Norwegian Claims Case*, Scott, *Hague Court Reports*, II, p. 39, at pp. 64, 65; *Corrie* Claim, *Opinions*, I, p. 213, at pp. 214, 215, 217; Nielsen, pp. 159-160; *Venables* Case, *Opinions*, I, p. 331, at pp. 344, 366-367; Nielsen, p. 205, at pp. 224-225; *Debenture Holders of San Marcos and Pinos Co.* Claim, *Decisions*, II, p. 135, at pp. 139, 140; *Mexican Tramways Co.* Claim, *ibid.*, II, p. 184, at p. 189; *The Felix,* Moore, *International Arbitrations* (1898)—henceforth cited as Moore—III, p. 2800, at p. 2811; *Socony-Vacuum Oil Co.* Case, American-Turkish Claims, p. 369, at pp. 374, 382; *Singer Sewing Machine Co.* Case, *ibid.*, p. 490, at p. 491; *Malamatinis* Case, *ibid.*, p. 603, at p. 605; *Dickson Car Wheel Co.* Claim, *Opinions*, III, p. 175, at pp. 199, 202; Nielsen, p. 505, at p. 515; *International Fisheries Co.* Case, *Opinions*, III, p. 207, at pp. 241-242; Nielsen, p. 520, at p. 539; *Salem* Case, Nielsen, p. 698; *Company General of the Orinoco* Case, Ralston, *French-Venezuelan Arbitrations* (1902), p. 244.

See also Lapradelle and Politis, *Recueil des Arbitrages internationaux* (2 Vols. 1932)—henceforth cited as Lapradelle and Politis—II, pp. 258-259 (note doctrinale); *American Bottle Co.* Claim, *Opinions*, II, p. 162; Nielsen, p. 339, at p. 340; *Pomeroy's El Paso Transfer Co.* Case, Nielsen, p. 418, at p. 420; *Parker Case, Opinions*, I, p. 35; *Peerless Motor Car Co.* Case, *ibid.*, p. 303; *United Dredging Co.* Case, *ibid.*, p. 394; *National Paper & Type Co.* Case, *Opinions*, II, p. 3; *Parsons Trading Co.* Case, *ibid.*, p. 135; *P.C.I.J., Ser. A. No. 20*, pp. 18-20 (*Serbian Loans* Case); *P.C.I.J., Ser. A/B, No. 76*, p. 18 (*Panevezys Saldutiskis Ry.* Case); Hudson, *ibid., Ser. A/B, No. 78*, p. 184 (*Société Commerciale de Belgique*); *ibid., Ser. B, No. 6*, p. 28 (*German Settlers in Poland*); *P.C.I.J., Ser. A, No. 7*, at p. 42 (*German Interests in Poland*), but see *Ser. A/B No. 77*, p. 107 (per Urrutia, dissenting *Electricity Co. of Sofia*); Genet, *Revue générale de droit international public*, 36 (1929), pp. 682-685.

44. Lipstein (1942), 27 *Transactions of the Grotius Society*, 142-176; (1944), 29 *ibid.*, 51-81; (1959), 8 *International and Comparative Law Quarterly*, 506, at p. 522; Schnitzer in *Recueil d'Etudes de droit international en hommage de P. Guggenheim* (1968), 702.

The following cases should now be added:

Diverted Cargoes Case, *International Law Reports* 1955, 820; (1956), 5 *International and Comparative Law Quarterly, 471*; *Rev. crit. d.i.p.* 1956, 278; *Ann. français de droit international* 1956, 427; *Rev. Arb.* 1956, 15.

Alsing Case (1954), (1956) 23 *International Law Reports* 633; (1959), 8 *International and Comparative Law Quarterly*, 320 with comments by Schwebel.

Aramco Case (1958), 27 *International Law Reports*, pp. 117 at 153 ff.; *Rev. crit. d.i.p.* 1963, 272; Batiffol *ibid.* 1964, 647; Bastid, *Ann. français dr. internat.* 1961, 300.

Sapphire Case (1963), 35 *International Law Reports*, pp. 136 ff., esp. 170 ff.; Lalive *Ann. suisse de dr. internat.* 19, (1962), 273; (1964), 13 *International & Comp. Law Quarterly*, 1011 (text in part); Lalive *ibid.*, 987; *Texaco/Calasiatic* v. *Government of Libya, Clunet* 1971, 350; Lalive *ibid.*, 319; *B.P.* v. *Libyan Arab Republic* (1979), 53 *International Law Reports* 297, 326 (Part VII, 1); and see European Convention on International Commercial Arbitration, Geneva, 21 August 1961, art. VII, *U.N. Treaty Series* vol. 484, (1963-64), 364, 374.

45. Moore, IV, p. 4181, at p. 4182; see also *Eldridge*'s Case, *ibid.*, p. 3460, at p. 3462.

46. See Lipstein, *Transactions of the Grotius Society*, 27 (1942), p. 142, especially at pp. 149-156.

47. *Cameron's* Claim, *Decisions*, I, p. 33, at p. 45; see also the *Pinson* Case, decided by the Franco-Mexican Claims Commission, *Revue générale de droit international public*, 39 (1932), p. 230, at p. 556 (43).

48. *P.C.I.J., Ser. A, No. 20*, pp. 41, 46; *ibid., No. 21*, pp. 124-125.

Erades in "De Conflictu Legum", *Essays presented to Kollewijn and Offerhaus* (1962), 145.

49. (1942), 27 *Transactions of the Grotius Society*, pp. 156-157; see also the *Norwegian Claims* Case, Scott, *Hague Court Reports*, II, p. 38, at pp. 64, 65. See also Kaeckenbeeck, *The International Experiment of Upper Silesia* (1942), p. 75, and n. 3, p. 78; Niboyet, *Répertoire de droit international*, Vol. 10 (1931), s.v. *ordre public*, especially Nos. 439-457.

50. Moore, *International Arbitrations*, IV (1898), p. 4349; Lapradelle and Politis, *Recueil des Arbitrages internationaux*, I (1932), 686, and see the *note doctrinale, ibid.*, p. 705, at pp. 707-709. See also, to the same effect the decisions of the same tribunal in *The Hermosa*, Moore, IV, p. 4374; Lapradelle and Politis, I, p. 688; *The Creole*, Moore, IV, p. 4375; Lapradelle and Politis, *loc. cit.* But see *The Comet, The Encomium*, Moore, IV, 4349; Lapradelle and Politis, I, p. 691, to the contrary seeing that the acts complained of occurred prior to the passing of the Act of 3 and 4 Wm. IV, c. 73.

51. Moore, *loc. cit.*, at pp. 4362-4365.

52. Moore, *loc. cit.*, at p. 4373.

53. Moore, *loc. cit.*, at p. 4361. But see the dissenting opinion of Hornby, the British Commissioner, *loc. cit.*, at pp. 4362-4372.

54. Moore, V, p. 5034; Lapradelle and Politis, I, p. 704; and see the *note doctrinale* by Strisower, *ibid.*, pp. 707-709, where he distinguishes between public policy in international law and municipal law. See also the dissenting opinion of Mr. Little in *Henry Woodruff and Flanagan, Bradley, Clark & Co.* v. *Venezuela*, Moore, IV, p. 3566; *Beales, Nobles Garrison* v. *Venezuela*, Moore, IV, p. 3548, at p. 3560; see also *Camy* v. *U.S.*, Moore, III, p. 2398, at p. 2400.

55. (1927), 8 *British Year Book of International Law*, 156, at p. 158; (1928), 22 *American Journal of International Law*, 404, at p. 407.

56. *Dusenberg* v. *Mexico*, Moore, III, p. 2157, at p. 2158; *Knox* v. *Mexico, ibid.*, III, p. 2166; *Robert* v. *Mexico, ibid.*, III, p. 2468, at p. 2471; *Rivlin, Guardian of H. Sternberg* v. *Turkey*, American-Turkish Claims, p. 622, at p. 626 (domicile characterised according to American notions); *Raeburn* v. *Mexico, Decisions*, II, p. 54, at p. 59 (domicile characterised according to English law); *Gleadell* v. *Mexico, ibid., I*, p. 55, at pp. 57, 63 (personal property, situs of choses in action characterised according to English law); *The Enterprize*, Moore, IV, p. 4349, at p. 4366 (rights over slaves characterised according to American notions); *Norwegian Claims* Case, Scott, *Hague Court Reports*, II, p. 38, at p. 67. But see *P.C.I.J., Ser. B, No. 10* at pp. 19-22, where the Court had to interpret private law

terms contained in a treaty. For a discussion of this problem see (1942), 27 *Transactions of the Grotius Society*, 158, and the literature quoted, *ibid*., p. 84. And see Niboyet, *Hague Rec.* 31 (1930 I), pp. 68-99; *ibid*., 40 (1932 II), pp. 180 ff.; Kaeckenbeeck, *loc. cit.* (above p. 69, n. 49), pp. 51, 61; Jenks (1938), 19 *British Year Book of International Law*, 67, at p. 84.

57. *The Montijo*, Moore, II, p. 1421, at p. 1430; *Raeburn* v. *Mexico, Decisions*, II, p. 54, at p. 55.

58. *P.C.I.J., Ser. A, No. 21*, at p. 124; see also *P.C.I.J., Ser. A, No. 7*, at p. 19 *(German Interests in Upper Silesia).*

59. *P.C.I.J., Ser. A, No. 20*, p. 46; see also the observations of Anzilotti, *P.C.I.J., Ser. A, No. 65*, at pp. 63-64 *(Danzig Legislative Decrees).*

60. But see the dissenting opinions of Bustamente, *P.C.I.J., Ser. A, No. 20*, at pp. 54-58; *ibid., No. 21*, at pp. 131-136, and of Pessoa, *ibid., No. 20*, at pp. 71 ff., especially at pp. 73-74; *ibid., No. 21*, at pp. 148-152. For the uncertainty of French law on the question in issue see Genet, *Revue générale de droit international*, 36 (1929), pp. 685-688. And see the *Lighthouse* Case *(France* v. *Greece), P.C.I.J., Ser. A/B, No. 62*, pp. 19-24, where the Court applied Turkish law. But see the observations of Judge Hudson in *P.C.I.J., Ser. A/B, No. 78*, p. 184 *(Société Générale de Belgique).* See also Jenks in (1938), 19 *British Year Book of International Law*, p. 67, at pp. 69, 89.

61. *Cook* v. *Mexico, Opinions*, II, p. 162, at p. 165; Nielsen, *International Law applied to Reclamations* (1933), p. 500, at p. 503; *Re Donnell's Executors, Re Hollins and McBlair*, Moore, IV, pp. 3545-3546.

62. *Reparation Commission* v. *U.S.A.* (1927), 8 *British Year Book of International Law*, 156, at p. 159; (1928), 22 *American Journal of International Law*, 404, at p. 408.

63. *Dr Baldwin's* Case, Moore, IV, p. 2859, at p. 2864.

64. Moore, I, p. 250, at 259; Lapradelle and Politis, II, p. 513, at p. 515, with a *note doctrinale* at p. 520.

65. Moore, I, p. 262, at p. 264; Lapradelle and Politis, II, p. 503, at p. 511.

66. See (1944), 29 *Transactions of the Grotius Society*, 51, at pp. 57-58, and notes 13-15 with cases.

67. See *ibid*., pp. 58-59, and notes 16-22 with cases.

68. See *ibid*., pp. 59-60, and note 23 with cases.

69. Nielsen, p. 390, at pp. 395-396; see also *Thomas Morrison* v. *Mexico*, Moore, III, p. 2325, at p. 2326; *P.C.I.J., Ser. A, No. 20*, p. 17 (*Serbian Loans* Case); *P.C.I.J., Ser. A/B, No. 61*, p. 232 (*Peter Pázmány University Case*).

70. (1944), 29 *Transactions of the Grotius Society*, 51, at pp. 60-61, and notes 24-30 with cases.

71. *Ibid*., pp. 61-62, and notes 31-33 with cases.

72. *Ibid*., pp. 69-71, and notes 65-79 with cases.

73. *Ibid*., pp. 71-72, and notes 80-85 with cases.

74. *Ibid*., pp. 72-73, and notes 86-98 with cases.

75. *Ibid*., p. 73, and notes 99-102 with cases.

76. *Ibid*., pp. 73-74, and notes 103-107 with cases.

77. *Ibid*., pp. 74-76, and notes 108-121 with cases.

78. If restricted to principles common to the legal systems of both parties, this provision amounts to no more than a call for cumulating the two legal systems concerned.

79. For this problem see *Abu Dhabi* case, *International Law Reports* 1951, Case No. 37; *Petroleum Development (Quatar) Ltd.* v. *Ruler of Quatar*, *International Law Reports* 1951, Case No. 38; *Ruler of Quatar* v. *International Marine Oil Ltd*, *International Law Reports* 1953, p. 534; see also Lena Goldfields Arbi-

tration, *Annual Digest of International Law Cases* (1929-30), Case No. 1; (1930), 34 *Cornell Law Quarterly*, 42; *Société Européenne d'Etudes et d'Entreprises* v. *Federal Popular Republic of Yugoslavia, Clunet* 1959, 1075. For lit. see McNair (1975), 31 *British Year Book of International Law*, 1; Mann (1944), 21 *ibid.*, 11 ff.; (1959), 35 *ibid.*, 34; (1967) 42 *ibid.*, 1, at pp. 2 ff.; in *Jus et Lex, Festgabe für Gutzwiller* (1959), 465; (1960) 54 *American Journal of International Law*, 572. Peyrefitte, *D.* 1965 Chron., 113; Level, *Comité français de d.i.p.*, 27 (1966), 209. See also *Davies Case* (*U.S.* v. *Mexico*), *Opinions*, I, p. 197, at p. 201; Nielsen, p. 145, at p. 148.

80. See Lipstein in *Rabels Z.*, 27 (1962), 359, at p. 361.

81. Mann (1943), 59 *Law Quarterly Review*, 42, 155; (1954), 70 *ibid.*, 217; (1955) 40 *Transactions of the Grotius Society*, 25; (1965), 51 *Virginia Law Rev.*, 604; *Hague Rec.* 132 (1971 I), 109, at pp. 145-156; Lipstein (1950), 35 *Transactions of the Grotius Society*, 157-188; Stevenson (1951), 51 *Col.L.R.*, 710; Zander (1959), 53 *American Journal of International Law*, 826; Greig (1967), 83 *Law Quarterly Review*; Bernstein (1967), 65 *Mich.L.R.*, 924; Sauveplanne, *Nederlands Tijdschrift voor Internationaal Recht*, 7 (1960), 17; Simmonds (1965), 14 *International and Comparative Law Quarterly*, 452. Leslie (1974), *Juridical Review*, 127.

82. Oppenheim, *International Law* (7 ed. 1948), Vol. I, p. 133, and note 2, p. 296.

83. [1921] 3 K.B. 532 (C.A.).

84. *Banco Nacional de Cuba* v. *Sabbatino*, 376 US 398; 11 L.ed. 2d 804 (1964).

85. See, e.g., Kegel in Sörgel, *Kommentar zum BGB*, Vol. 7 (10 ed. 1970), para. 101, before Art. 7, EGBGB, and note 1 with lit.; Wengler, *Festschrift für Lewald* (1953), 615-632; Sauveplanne, *loc. cit.*, p. 23 ff., and the Civil Court of Rome, 13 Sept. 1954 in *Anglo-Iranian Oil Co. Ltd* v. *S.U.P.O.R. Co.*, 1955 *International Law Reports* 23, at p. 42, with cases, notes 1-3; *Foro it.*, 1955, I, 256; *Riv. dir. int.*, 39 (1955), p. 97. The judgment of the Civil Court of Antwerp of 21 February 1939, *Annual Digest* 1938-1940, Case No. 11; *La Belgique Judiciaire*, 1939, Nos. 11, 12 col. 371; that of the Court of Appeal of Arnhem of 12 June 1939; *Annual Digest* 1919-1942 (Suppl. vol.), 19 *W. & N.J.* 1940, No. 20, and of the District Court of New York (S.D.) of 13 April 1939, *Ann. Dig.* 1938-1940, Case No. 35, 28 F. Supp. 279 definitely deny that any court is entitled to decide on the lawfulness of an expropriation carried out by a foreign government; the same conclusion was reached by the Court of Tokyo in its judgment of 21 September 1953, 1953 *International Law Reports* 305.

See also (1957), 1 *Japanese Annual of International Law* 55 (District Court, Tokyo, 27 May 1953). For France see now: Cass. 3 May 1973, *G.P.* 1973. 2.860; *Clunet* 1974, 859; *D.S.* 1973 I.R. 150; *J.C.P.* 1973. IV. 218; *Rev. crit. d.i.p.* 1974, 727 on appeal from Paris, 8 July 1970 (unpublished?), and from Trib.Gr. Inst. Seine, 12 Jan. 1966, *Rev. crit. d.i.p.* 1967, 120; *J.C.P.* 1967.II.15266; Paris 23 April 1931, *Clunet* 1931, 1117; but contrast Trib.Seine 11 June 1921, *S.* 1924.2.9; 12 December 1923, *G.P.* 1924.1.96, 100, *Clunet* 1924, 133; 9 May 1925, *Clunet* 1926, 127; Aix 23 December 1925, *G.P.* 1926.1.169; *Clunet* 1926, 667 on appeal from Trib.Com. Marseilles, 23 April 1925, *G.P.* 1925.2.169 with a note referring to other cases; Paris 30 April 1926, *G.P.* 1926.2.30, *Clunet* 1926, 944; Seine 24 December 1926, *Rev. de droit international privé* 1928, 97; Batiffol and Lagarde, *Droit international privé I* (6 ed. 1974), no. 256 p. 327 ff. For Switzerland see now the Federal Tribunal, 30 March 1965, BGE 91 II 117, 132. And see Kralik, *Z.f.R.V.* 3 (1962) 75, 77; Schwind, *Handbuch des Oesterreichischen Internationalen Privatrechts* (1975) p. 43 n. 13 with ref. to cases.

86. See, e.g., *Anglo-Iranian Oil Co. Ltd* v. *S.U.P.O.R.*, Civil Court of Rome,

13 Sept. 1954, 1955 *International Law Reports*, 23, 25; *Foro it.* 1955, I, 256; *Riv. dir. int.*, 39 (1955), 97.

87. This may have been the ground for the decision in *Duke of Brunswick* v. *King of Hanover* (1848), 2 H.L.C.I. at pp. 17, 21, 27, discussed by Mann, *Hague Rec.* 132 (1971 I), at pp. 145-146.

88. See Mann, *loc. cit.*, p. 152.

89. *Buron* v. *Denman* (1848), 2 Ex. 167; see Mann, *loc. cit.*, p. 156, but see Sauveplanne, p. 33.

90. See also Mann, *loc. cit.*, pp. 151, 153, 156; it is certainly not a principle of Public International Law.

91. [1921] 3 K.B. 532.

92. Per Warrington L.J. at pp. 548-549: territoriality of laws; Bankes, L.J. at p. 545: *lex situs*; Scrutton L.J. at pp. 555, 556, 558, 559: sovereign immunity and a restrictive application of public policy by the forum. See Lipstein, *loc. cit.*, p. 158.

93. (1878) 96 U.S. 176.

94. An *obiter dictum* suggests that the legislation of a de facto recognised government would, in general, have been recognised.

95. (1897) 168 U.S. 250.

96. (1918), 246 U.S. 297. See also *Ricaud* v. *American Leather Co.* (1918), 246 U.S. 304, 310: "It is irrelevant whether the property was owned by an American or a foreign national". H. Lauterpacht [1954], *Cambridge Law Journal*, 20, seeks to draw a distinction according as the objects of the executive measure are nationals of the foreign country or not, referring to *Princess Paley Olga v. Weiss* [1929], 1 K.B. 718. This distinction is not only unsupported by the authorities, but it would lead to the result that in the case of a violation of Public International Law by foreign law which is normally applicable, the rule of foreign law would have to be disregarded where nationals of the country of the *forum*, possibly where nationals of third countries, but never where stateless persons or nationals of the country of the *lex causae* are involved. Such a discriminatory application of local public policy does violence to the notion of public policy itself. Cp. *Banque des Marchands de Moscou (Koupetschesky), Royal Assurance Association* v. *The Liquidator* [1952], 1 All E.R. 1269; [1951], 1 T.L.R. 739. See also, e.g., *Koh-i-Noor, L. H. Hardtmuth* v. *Koh-i-Noor Tužkárna L. H. Hardmuth* decided by the Austrian Supreme Court on 2 June 1958, *SZ* XXXI (1958), p. 280; 26 *International Law Reports*, 40.

97. (1897), 168 U.S. 250.

98. This need to make a preliminary choice of law is now acknowledged by the decision in *Tabacalera Severiano Jorge S.A.* v. *Standard Cigar Co.*, 392 F. 2d 706, 714 (5. Cir. 1968), cert. denied, 393 U.S. 924, 21. L.ed. 2d 260 (1968).

99. 376 U.S. 398, 11 L.ed. 2d 804 (1964); the literature is enormous; here it is only necessary to add Hopkins [1964], *Cambridge Law Journal*, 282; *Banco Nacional de Cuba* v. *Farr, Whitlock & Co.*, 383 F. 2d 166 (1967), cert. denied, 390 U.S. 956, 19 L.ed. 2d 1151 (1968).

100. 78 Stat. 1013, am. 79 Stat. 653, 22 U.S.C. § 2370 (e) (2).

101. See Stone C.J. (diss.) in *U.S.* v. *Pink* (1942), 315 U.S. 203, at p. 252. But see, e.g., *The Maret*, 145 F.Ld 431 (5. Circ.); (1944-1945), 58 *Harv.L.R.*, 612; (1944-1945) 93 *Univ. of Pennsylvania L.R.*, 323; and cp. *Carl Zeiss Stiftung* v. *Carl Zeiss V.E.B.*, 293 F. Supp. 892 at p. 900-901, 915-916; affd. 433 F. 2d 686, 699 (2 Cir. 1970).

102. See also Bernstein (1967), 65 *Mich.L.R.*, 924.

103. See Lipstein (1950), 35 *Transactions of the Grotius Society*, 157, at pp. 183-187.

104. See *Carl Zeiss Stiftung Ltd* v. *Rayner and Keeler*, [1967] 1 A.C. 853, but see

the observations of Lord Reid at p. 906 and of Lord Wilberforce at pp. 953, 954. And see now *Hesperides Hotels Ltd* v. *Aegean Turkish Holidays Ltd* [1978], Q.B. 205, 216, 218, approved [1979], A.C. 588 on other grounds; see also Neuhaus *German Yearbook of International Law*, 21 (1978), 60 at 67 n. 35; Raape-Sturm, *Internationales Privatrecht* I (1977), 45, 310.

105. See above, p. 74, n. 85 and see Lipstein, *loc. cit.*, p. 185; Sauveplanne (above p. 183, n. 81), at p. 21, with cases notes 17, 20, 24, 46; *Carl Zeiss Stiftung* v. *V.E.B.C. Zeiss Jena*, 293 F. Supp. 892, 900-901, 915-916 (1968), (1969) 63 *Am. J. of International Law*, 638; (1969), 3 *Int. Lawyer*, 525; (1968), *U.S. P.Q.*, 97; Treves, *Rev. crit. d.i.p.*, 1967, p. 23; *Riv. dir. int. priv. e proc.*, 3 (1967), 437; 6 (1970), 451, with references to the practice of the courts in continental Europe; affd. 433 F. 2d 686, 699 (2 Cir. 1970); Bernstein (1972), 20 *American Journal of Comparative Law*, 299.

106. See, e.g., *The Miriella*, decided by the Tribunal of Venice on 11 March 1953, *Foro it.*, 1953, I, 719, 721, 1955 *International Law Reports*, 19, 21.

107. [1921], 3 K.B. 532.

108. See Lipstein (1967), 42 *British Year Book of International Law*, 265-270, and notes 2 and 3 with lit.; for the cases see p. 268 and notes 2-8; and see Mann, *Hague Rec.* 132 (1971 I), 151-152; Batiffol, *Aspects philosophiques du droit international privé* (1956), p. 114, n. 1; Niboyet, *Revue de droit international et de législation comparé* 1928, 753; *Traité de droit international privé français*, III (1944), nos. 978-980, pp. 403-408; De Nova, *Rev. crit. d.i.p.* 1948, 534; Vitta, *Diritto Internazionale Privato*, I (1972), 237-240; Union Internationale des Magistrats, *Nederlands Tijdschrift voor Internationaal Recht*, 19 (1972), 81, 83; Siehr, *Foro italiano* 1975, V, 7. But see critically Kahn-Freund, "International Law and Economic Order", *Essays in Honour of F.A. Mann* (1977), 207; and restrictively Bay.ObLG, 21 February 1969, NJW 1969, 988; *IPRspr.* 1968-1969, No. 106 at p. 247 (c); OLG Hamm, 29 November 1969, *IPRspr.* 1968-1969, No. 113 at p. 266 with references.

109. See, e.g., the Constitution of the German Federal Republic, Arts. 25, 100; of Italy, Arts. 101, 134-136; of Austria, Arts. 9, 140, 140a.

110. See, e.g., the Constitutions of the German Federal Republic, Art. 100, subject to the exception of "Inzidente Normen Kontrolle", and of Italy, Art. 134, and of Austria, Art. 89.

111. For a rejection of this view see, *inter alia*, Mann, above p. 75, n. 90.

112. See, e.g., H. Lauterpacht [1954], *Cambridge Law Journal*, 20; Mann (1954), 70 *Law Quarterly Review*, 181; (1956), 19 *Modern Law Rev.*, 301; Mann, *Hague Rec.* 132 (1971 I), 107, 154; Morgenstern (1951), 4 *International Law Quarterly*, 327, 340; O'Connell (1955), 4 *International and Comparative Law Quarterly*, 267; M. Mann (1956), 5 *International and Comparative Law Quarterly*, 245; E. Lauterpacht, *ibid.*, p. 301; Lipstein [1956], *Cambridge Law Journal*, 138; de Nova, *Rev. crit. d.i.p.*, 47 (1958), 519, 534; Gihl in *Liber Amicorum ... to Bagge*, 56; Kollewijn, *Nederlands Tijdschrift voor Internationaal Recht*, 6 (1959), 140; Schwarzenberger (1960), 9 Journal of Public Law (Emory University), 147, at p. 164; Mann, *Neue Juristische Wochenschrift* 1961, 705; Seidl-Hohenveldern, in Recht im Wandel, *Festschrift Carl Heymanns Verlag* (1966), pp. 591-619.

113. *The Rose Mary, Anglo-Iranian Oil Co.* v. *Jaffrate*, decided on 9 January 1953 by the Supreme Court of Aden [1953], 1 W.L.R. 246; 1953 *International Law Reports*, 316; (1953) 47 *American Journal of International Law*, 325; *Clunet* 1956, 713, and the decisions of lower German courts cited there.

114. See above, p. 77, n. 106.

115. See above, pp. 77-78; only when the law in question has been pro-

mulgated, or the executive measure has been executed by an Occupying Power, courts in other countries must look exclusively to Public International Law in order to determine the validity of the law or measure; see Lipstein, *Communicazioni e Studi,* IV (1952), 114-141.

116. Gamillscheg, *Festschrift für Nipperdey* (1965), I, p. 323; *Gesetz über das Bundesverfassungsgericht* of 12 March 1951 (BGBl. 1951, I, p. 423, para. 13 (6), (11), (12)); Decision of the Federal Constitutional Court, 1 (1951), p. 11; 6 (1957), pp. 291, 295; 31, 58, 80-85; Morelli, *Studi Perassi* (1957), II, 169, at pp. 180-186; Mosconi, *Diritto internazionale,* 14 (1960), 426 at pp. 429, 435, restricts the effect of Art. 10 of the Italian Constitution incorporating the supremacy of international law to the control of Italian legislation.

117. England: *Re Helbert Wagg & Co. Ltd* [1956], Ch. 323, 344.

Italy: *The Miriella, Anglo-Iranian Oil Co.* v. *Società Petrolifera Orientale,* decided by the Tribunal of Venice on 11 March 1953, *Giur. it.* 1953, I, 2, 305; *Foro it.* 1953, I, 719; *Riv. dir. internaz.,* 36 (1953), 217; 1955 *International Law Reports,* 19; (1953), 2 *Internat. and Comp. L.Q.,* 628; *Anglo-Iranian Oil Co.* v. *S.U.P.O.R.,* decided by the Civil Court of Rome on 13 September 1954, *Giur. it.,* 1955, I, 2, 91, *Foro it., 1955,* I, 256; *Riv. dir. internaz.,* 38 (1955), 97; *Rev. crit. d.i.p.,* 47 (1948), 519, 1955 *International Law Reports,* 23; Cass. 19 February 1960; *Kooh-i-Noor Tuzkarna* v. *L. & C. Hardtmuth, Foro it.,* 1960, I, 985, *Riv. dir. internaz.,* 43 (1960), 533; 40 *International Law Reports,* 17; *Svit Impresa Nazionale* v. *Cipera,* decided by the Court of Appeal of Bologna on 28 April 1956, *Riv. dir. internaz.,* 40 (1957) 264. But see now more negatively: *Texaco Overseas Petroleum Co. & California Asiatic Oil Co.* v. *Montedison S.p.A. et al.,* decided 10 November 1976 by the Italian Court of Cassation (United Sections), *Riv. dir. int. priv. e proc.,* 14 (1978), 98.

Germany: *N.V. Vereenigde Deli Maatschappijen N.V. Senembah Mij.* v. *Deutsche-Indonesische Tabak Ges.,* decided by the C.A. Bremen, on 21 August 1959, *Archiv für Völkerrecht,* 9 (1961), 318, at pp. 352-355; *Jahrbuch für Internationales Recht,* 9 (1960), 84, 28 *International Law Reports,* 16.

France: Cass. 23 April 1969, *Crédit Foncier d'Algérie* v. *Narbonne, Clunet* 1969, 914, see also *Revue crit. d.i.p.,* 1969, 917; 1970, 754.

Netherlands: *Bank of Indonesia* v. *Senembah Maatschappij* decided 4 June 1959 by the Court of Appeal of Amsterdam, *N.J.* 1959, No. 350, *Nederlands Tijdschrift voor Internationaal Recht,* 8 (1961), 79; 30 (1960), *International Law Reports,* 28, on appeal from a decision of the President of the District Court, Amsterdam, dated 22 December 1958, *N.J.* 1959, No. 73, *Nederlands Tijdschrift,* 7 (1960), 285, 403, *N.J.* 1959, p. 73 (1958 II), *International Law Reports,* 38; *Clark* v. *Bank voor Handel en Scheepvaart,* decided by the Dutch Supreme Court on 17 October 1969, *N.J.* 1969, p. 279, *International Legal Materials,* 9 (1970), 758.

Japan: *Anglo-Iranian Oil Co.* v. *Idemitsu Kosan Co.,* decided by the High Court, Tokyo in 1953 *International Law Reports,* 312; on appeal from District Court, Tokyo, 27 May 1953, *ibid.,* p. 305; *Japanese Annual of Internat. Law* 1957, 55.

118. *Bernstein* v. *Van Heyghen,* 163 F. 2d 246 (1947), cert. denied, 332 U.S. 772; 92 L.ed. 357 (1947); Mann, *Hague Rec.* 132 (1971 I), at pp. 149-150, 154, but see to the contrary *Bernstein* v. *N.V. Nederlandsche Amerikaansche, etc.,* 210 F. 2d. 375 (2 Cir. 1954), approved by the Supreme Court in *First National City Bank* v. *Banco Nacional de Cuba,* 406 U.S. 759, 32 L.ed. 2d 466 (1972), rehearing denied 409 U.S. 887, 34 L.ed. 2d 155 (1972). As regards England: *Frankfurter* v. *Exner* [1947], Ch. 629, on the ground that the measure was penal; see also *Novello* v. *Hinrichsen* [1951], Ch. 595, 1026.

119. For exceptions see below, No. 59, pp. 99-102.

120. Evrigenis, *Hague Rec.* 118 (1966 II), at pp. 410-422; Ehrenzweig, *Private International Law* (1967), pp. 57-74, ss. 21-29.

121. Kahn-Freund, *The Growth of Internationalism in English Private International Law* (1962).

122. Graveson, *Rev. crit. d.i.p.*, 1962, 397; (1964), 78 *L.Q.R.*, 337; *XXth Century Comparative and Conflicts Law* (1961), 307.

123. See, e.g., Pillet, *Principes*, p. 253, No. 110; p. 255, No. 112; but see p. 250; Batiffol, *Aspects philosophiques ...*, p. 118, n. 53, note 1 with references to modern Italian literature.

124. See in addition to the writers quoted above in n. 123, Unger (1957), 43 *Transactions of the Grotius Society*, 87, at p. 94.

125. See below, Nos. 53-54, pp. 93-94.

126. See below, No. 59, pp. 99-102.

127. E.g., Italy, Introductory Provisions to the Civil Code, Art. 30.

128. See above Nos. 29-39, and in particular Ehrenzweig, above Nos. 29-30, pp. 30-32.

129. See [1972 B], *Cambridge Law Journal*, 67, at p. 76.

130. See below, p. 125.

PART III. THE STRUCTURE AND INTERPRETATION OF RULES OF PRIVATE INTERNATIONAL LAW

Section 26. Structure

53. Ideally, every individual rule of Private Law should be served by its own rules of Private International Law or it should disclose its territorial or personal limitations.[1] The immense variety of rules of substantive law makes this a practical impossibility and the parallel existence of such unilateral rules of Private International Law spread among a multitude of countries would create intractable problems of overlaps and lacunae which only an overriding international system of choice of law could solve. Instead two techniques are employed, one general, one particular. The former is represented by the ordinary rules of Private International Law which may be unilateral by indicating directly only when the *lex fori* applies, or bilateral by using criteria which lead at times to the application of the *lex fori* and at times to that of other legal systems. In effect this technique always leads in the end to a system of rules which ensure the application of the *lex fori* or of foreign law in clearly determined circumstances. The latter is exceptional and is represented by the so-called "spatially conditioned internal rules" [2] or "legislatively localised laws",[3] "particular choice of law rules" [4] or "functionally restricting rules".[5]

54. *Operative Facts and Connecting Factors.* Usually sets of rules of substantive law are grouped together for the purpose of formulating one broad principle of Private International Law. This method of grouping adopts largely the time-honoured categories which were applied by the statutists. Today, however, these categories are no longer employed to describe the nature of the substantive law which claims to apply in space. Instead, the categories are detached from the rules of substantive law. They have come into their own, have spawned new categories and now form the backbone of the modern independent rules of Private International Law. Nevertheless, their character has remained the same, and they are still few in number. They concern status,[6] capacity, marriage, divorce and judicial separation, nullity of marriage, maintenance, guardianship and adoption, corporations,[7] contracts,[8] quasi-contracts, torts,[9] interests in movables and in immovables,[10] formalities and procedure.

For want of a better expression these heads of typical legal situations will be called *operative facts*.[11]

These operative facts are linked to a particular system of domestic law by means of what are called *connecting factors*.[12] These are limited too and can be enumerated without difficulty. They are:

Nationality, domicile, residence, ordinary residence,[13] habitual residence,[14] place of contracting, place of performance, the place of the situation of the object, the intention of the parties, the centre of a relationship, the place where a transaction is concluded and the locality of the court seized of the dispute. Normally a rule of Private International Law consists of one set of operative facts and one connecting factor.[15] Sometimes one set of operative facts is coupled with two connecting factors which may function cumulatively [16] or alternatively.[17]

Section 27. Interpretation

55. *Interpretation of Connecting Factors.* Like all rules of law, the rules of Private International Law require interpretation. This task is simple where it is limited to the connecting factors. It is highly complex when it involves the operative facts.

Each connecting factor indicates a particular legal system which is to apply to the individual legal situation. Since Private International Law is domestic law and forms part of the *lex fori*, it follows that the *lex fori* alone determines in what circumstances foreign law is to apply. Consequently, not only the selection of the appropriate connecting factor, but also its interpretation, is exclusively determined by the *lex fori*. Thus in an English court the question whether a person resident in France is domiciled there must be decided according to English and not according to French notions.[18] The place where a contract is concluded is fixed, in an English court, where and when the acceptance is posted, even if according to the law of the country where it was dispatched, it takes effect only where and when the offeror receives it.[19]

Three exceptions must be noted, however. In the first place the connecting factor nationality must be interpreted in accordance with the law of the country of which the person concerned is alleged to be a national. In the second place, connecting factors, such as habitual residence, which have been received into the domestic Private International Law of countries as a result of the adoption of an International Convention,[20] should, it is submitted, be interpreted with special regard to uniformity.[21] In the third place, in all cases involving *renvoi*, when the forum applies foreign law including foreign Private International Law, the connecting factors of the foreign rules of Private International Law must be interpreted in accordance with the law of the foreign country.[22]

56. *Interpretation of Operative Facts—Characterisation.* The same process of characterisation, which relies on the *lex fori*, may also seem natural in any legal system when it comes to the interpretation of the operative facts [23] and is seemingly imperative in those legal systems where the courts are believed to be called upon to apply foreign law of their own motion to a set of facts pleaded by the parties.[24] In reality, so it would appear, no suit involving a foreign element is introduced in which the plaintiff (and subsequently the defendant) has not considered his rights (or his defences) according to some legal system. Despite outward appearances, it does not seem to make any difference whether the court may, or is bound to, ascertain of its own motion (as courts in civil law countries can) whether and, if so, which system of laws applies, and what the particular rule of foreign law is which must be taken into consideration, or whether a party must plead not only the facts but also the law, if foreign, on which he intends to rely (as is the practice in common law countries).[25] The only difference appears to be that courts in civil law countries can, and courts in common law countries cannot, go beyond the allegations of the parties. The difference is one of degree only.[26]

In other words, cases raising a question of foreign law differ from purely domestic cases in the manner of their presentation. In purely domestic cases the facts are pleaded and a claim must be submitted. However, if the plaintiff or the defendant believes that foreign law is applicable he must introduce his claim in the light of some foreign law according to which he alleges to have a right against the defendant. The same applies to a defendant who may wish to plead that some other law—be it the *lex fori* or some other foreign legal system—applies and that according to the latter the claim is not well founded. The claim or defence must be framed in the light of a particular system of laws in order to induce the court to apply foreign law.[27] At this stage, proof of ordinary facts and proof of foreign law show different features. An allegation of foreign law forces the court to exercise a choice of law. The court, relying on its set of rules of conflict of laws, must ascertain which rule of its Private International Law covers the claim or defence.[28] Difficulties arise from the fact that the claim or defence is, *ex hypothesi*, expressed in substance and in form in terms of domestic law, primarily foreign. The operative facts of rules of Private International Law are formulated sometimes in terms of the domestic law of the *forum*,[29] but more frequently in terms peculiar to Private International Law; [30] yet the court must apply its own rules of Private International Law to claims presented in terms of foreign domestic law, if it is to determine whether the law pleaded by the party applies.[31] For this purpose each must be interpreted in terms of the other.[32] This process of subsuming claims formulated in accordance with one legal system under one of several rules of the conflict of laws of the forum by way of interpreting each in terms of the other is the essence of characterisation. The process of interpreting rules involving at least two, and possibly more, legal systems must necessarily rely on some legal notions, and over the years reliance on those of the *lex fori*, the *lex causae* and of comparative jurisprudence has been canvassed in turn. The present analysis must discard the approach from the *lex fori*, which assumes that facts alone must be characterised, and not facts presented in the light of some legal system.[33] However, the present analysis does not embrace the approach from the alleged *lex causae*, but it takes the *lex causae* into consideration.[34] According to the view set out here, abstract rules of law as such are not characterised. The courts analyse the nature of a claim (or defence) expressed according to some system of laws (foreign law or the *lex fori*), in the light of the function (not the technical connotation) of that rule within the particular legal system. They relate the claim or defence so analysed to that among their own rules of Private International Law which, upon a broad interpretation (not restricted to notions of the domestic law of the *forum*), is capable of covering the claim in question. This interpretation of disparate notions in terms of each other is the process of characterisation. The result is an indication of the law applicable which may, or may not, be that which has been pleaded by the party or parties.[35]

The process of characterisation set out here was expressed by the German Federal Supreme Court in these words:

> "The subsumption of these rules [i.e., Art. 992 of the Dutch Civil Code] must be made in accordance with German law. In this connection the following principles of interpretation must be observed; the rules of foreign law must be examined with a view to their meaning and purpose, they must be analysed from the standpoint of foreign law and they must be compared with the

institutions of the German legal order. On the basis of this knowledge, they must be subsumed by the German rules of Private International Law, the characteristics of which are shaped by the notions and delimitations of German law." [36]

It was in effect adopted on two recent occasions in England, although the process was not formulated in the terms submitted here.[37] Technically it involves one of three situations: either the claim or defence is identical in form and in substance with similar claims or defences in the *lex fori*,[38] or it is unknown in substance and in form in the *lex fori* [39] or it corresponds in form to a similar claim in the *lex fori*, but the formal similarity conceals a material difference.[40]

57. Although foreign law must only be alleged and proved once during the proceedings, it must be considered at two stages of the process of judicial reasoning. The first stage alone involves the process of interpretation known as characterisation or qualification. Here the court (whether in civil or common law countries) [41] must not only consider the facts but the individual rule or set of rules either of the *lex fori* or of foreign law on which the party relies and which are alleged to be applicable. Thus the Private International Law of the forum is at no stage concerned with a reference to foreign law in the abstract or with the categories of foreign law in general; it is concerned with a functional analysis of a particular rule within its own setting. Consequently during the second stage, which is exclusively concerned with the application of foreign law, no additional reliance is required on the characterisation of the foreign law as practised abroad by the courts of the country of the *lex causae* for the purpose of applying their own rules of Private International Law, except in situations involving *renvoi*. The reason is that, upon proper analysis, there is no need to reduce the foreign law applicable to concrete rules and to individualise the rules of foreign law a second time. They are individualised in the allegations or pleadings of the parties once and for all. As the process of characterisation is understood here, there is no place for secondary characterisation.[42]

In particular, it is of no importance that for technical reasons, due, *inter alia*, to the wording of a statute which requires unconditional and uniform application by the courts of its own country and is therefore regarded as procedural (on the illogical ground that all procedural laws require uniform unconditional application by the forum), such laws as Statutes of Frauds and Statutes of Limitations in common law countries are characterised as procedural. What matters is the function of the rule within its own setting: does it only affect the remedy, or does it also affect the right? [43]

Viewed from this angle, the famous sybilline riddles which have plagued the German Supreme Court, fascinated writers, and generally, occupied three generations of lawyers lose their glamour.

If German law regards limitation of actions as a matter of substance and refers to the law governing the contract, while the law of New York which governs it regards it as procedural, the latter formal characterisation is irrelevant, if the function of the New York rule is the same as that envisaged by the German rule of Private International Law.[44]

If (at a time when breach of promise was an actionable contractual claim in England),[45] parties entered into an engagement to marry each other, which was governed by French law, and a breach occurred in England (where the same act was a breach of contract), once again the function of each rule must be analysed. Such an analysis will show that, notwithstanding its delictual configuration, the French rule, like the English, serves to provide a remedy in a situation which is derived from an agreement, but which cannot be called "contractual" in France, given the reluctance of French law to admit that an engagement to marry could be enforceable (if only by granting damages). Thus an English court can treat a claim based on French law as contractual and apply French law.[46]

58. The prevalence of situations of this nature (characterisation of Statutes of Frauds, Statutes of Limitations) [47] in the practice of the courts in the United States may account for the unwillingness of modern American writers to concede to characterisation its proper function, which is real in those situations which arise only rarely in the United States, due to the close affinity of the legal systems within the Union, when a claim or defence is either unknown in form or in substance in the *lex fori*, or if it corresponds in form to a similar claim or defence in the *lex fori*, but the formal similarity conceals a material difference.[48]

At the same time, a greater readiness to acknowledge the more sophisticated function of characterisation, as understood here, could have enabled American courts to deal in a more orthodox manner, but with the same result, with cases such as *Babcock* v. *Jackson*.[49] Many obligations sounding at first sight in tort arise from or are affected by previous agreements which may include an express or implied choice of law clause.[50]

59. In contrast to ordinary rules of Private International Law, those called interchangeably spatially conditioned internal rules, legislatively localised laws, functionally restricting or self-limiting rules [51] determine the application *ratione personae* or *ratione loci* of particular rules of domestic law. Technically this is achieved by adding a personal or territorial restriction or extension to a particular rule of domestic law instead of formulating rules of the conflict of laws consisting of broad categories of operative facts (*supra* par. 54) which are then applied to claims formulated in accordance with some system of laws, whether it be foreign law or the domestic law of the court.[52]

Spatially conditioned or self-limiting rules do not necessarily exclude the application of foreign law and therefore differ quantitatively only, but not qualitatively from the unilateral rules of self-limitation discussed above [53] which circumscribe the operation of certain branches of domestic law, mostly described as forming part of public law. The latter, as well as a number of rules of a not clearly defined character which claim to apply peremptorily never contemplate the application of foreign law and have been described as *règles d'application immédiate* or *norme di applicazione necessaria.* Both types of rules must be distinguished from mandatory rules of domestic law. They, like their counterpart, directory rules (*droit supplétif*), apply only if called upon by the rules of the conflict of laws of the *lex fori.*[53a]

The interplay between ordinary rules of Private International Law and unilateral self-limiting rules of domestic public law can be observed in such situations as that underlying the *Boll* Case (*Netherlands* v. *Sweden*).[54] There the ordinary Dutch choice of law rule on guardianship clashed with a Swedish self-limiting rule on the protection of children in need of care. The application of ordinary rules of Private International Law coupled with the recognition of the operation abroad of foreign self-limiting rules of public law is a frequent practice.[55] The interplay between ordinary rules of Private International Law and spatially conditioned internal rules is much rarer.[56]

Spatially conditioned or self-limiting rules of the narrower and the broader kind must not be confused with statutory provisions containing a unilateral choice of law rule modifying a general rule of the conflict of laws, which may itself be unilateral in character. In the latter case a set of operative facts, such as legitimation by subsequent marriage, is linked to the *lex fori* by a connecting factor based e.g., on the nationality of, or on a domicile in, the country of the *forum*. Such rules are capable of bilateralisation so as to enable the *forum* to apply foreign law in equivalent circumstances, but not necessarily.

The Wills Act 1861 (Lord Kingsdown's Act), which applied in Great Britain until 1963, provides a good example. While the Act applied to wills of personality made by British subjects (and incidentally provided choice of law rules for them in those limited circumstances), the general rule of Private International Law, relying on the law of the last domicile, applied in all other circumstances, no matter whether the testator was domiciled in England or not.

The problem is more complicated, if the rules of Private International Law of the forum refer to foreign law, and the foreign law applicable contains either a unilateral rule of Private International Law or a spatially conditioned rule of domestic law. In the former case, the question is, first, whether the unilateral rule has been interpreted as a bilateral one and, if so, secondly, whether *renvoi* applies. If it has not been interpreted as a bilateral rule, and the case is not covered by the unilateral rule, the reference to foreign law remains one to foreign domestic law. If, however, the foreign domestic rule is a spatially conditioned rule a considerable difficulty arises.[57]

Spatially conditioned rules of the *lex fori* apply *propriis vigoribus*,[57a] irrespective of what law governs the issue. A foreign spatially conditioned statute or provision is not normally taken into account unless it forms part of the law governing the issue in accordance with the choice of law rules of the *lex fori*.[57b] If it forms part of the latter it can be argued that the provision applies irrespective of its own limitations on the ground that the initial reference to foreign law is final,[57c] but it may be objected that the applicable foreign law is thus falsified. An alternative approach must take two situations into consideration. If the foreign spatially conditioned rule is extensive and purports to apply in circumstances in which another legal system applies according to the rules of Private International Law of the *forum*, the claim to extend to the latter is disregarded.

If the foreign spatially conditioned rule is restrictive, it may be possible to disregard it and to apply the general law of the foreign *lex causae* [57d] in a subsidiary capacity. However, this may lead to strange solutions. If a French court dealing with the legitimacy of a child of a putative marriage entered into by a father, a citizen of the United Kingdom domiciled at all times in Spain, refers to the father's *lex patriae*, deemed to be English law, the Legitimacy Act 1959, s. 2, legitimating children of such void marriages does not apply, since it is restricted to fathers domiciled in England at the time of the child's birth (s. 2 (2)). Does the previous English law apply in these circumstances so as to render the child illegitimate? The wording of the statute suggests that the legislature did not wish to extend the operation of the Act to situations which according to English Private International Law are governed by the law of the father's foreign domicile, Spain. Can it be argued, therefore, that a problem of *renvoi* arises? [57e] It is believed that is does not. Although the seeming link is the feature that a spatially conditioned rule limits its own sphere of operation in some form or another, it does not constitute an abdication in favour of some other legal system. That function is fulfilled by the conflicts rules of the foreign *lex causae*. Instead, it only refuses to apply as part of its own system of law. Since any reliance on the previous law of the *lex causae* may display a touch of the unreal, only two alternatives remain: to apply the *lex fori* or the *lex causae,* stripped of its personal or territorial restriction. Of these two alternatives the latter is more attractive as being in accordance with the general approach to foreign spatially conditioned rules.

Sometimes it may be possible to detect a rule of Private International Law which refers to a legal system other than that of the *lex causae*; also spatially conditioned rules of domestic law are often special legislation, and if they do not apply, general rules of domestic law can be relied upon. Article 992 of the Dutch Civil Code (which states that Dutch nationals must make their wills in notarial form, even if the will is made abroad) and Article 170 of the French Civil Code (which requires French nationals marrying abroad to comply with certain formalities of French law) merely extend to situations abroad certain formal requirements of Dutch and French law concerning wills and marriages which apply peremptorily in the Netherlands and in France. Thus a reference by the Private International Law of the forum to Dutch or French law involving these articles as part of the *lex loci actus* or the *lex loci celebrationis* will mean a reference to Dutch or French law applicable to these formalities.[58] However, a spatially conditioned rule of domestic law may indicate the need to characterise the rule differently from a rule which is not spatially conditioned. Thus it has been contended that the requirement of form expressed in Article 992 of the Dutch Civil Code is to be characterised as one of substance, namely capacity to make a will, and it remained for the Hague Convention of 1961 on the Form of Wills [59] to exclude this practice.[60] The Carriage of Goods by Sea Act 1929 enacted in Great Britain and the

Carriage of Goods by Sea Ordinances of Palestine and Newfoundland, which provided the basis of the litigation in *The Torni* [61] and the *Vita Food Case* [62] concerned shipments out of these countries and left it to the ordinary rules of domestic law to solve questions arising under contracts of carriage by sea into Great Britain, Palestine and Newfoundland.[62a]

Section 29. Transposition, Substitution and Adaptation

60. *Transposition, substitution* and *adaptation,* first observed by continental writers,[63] are phenomena which can be found in all legal systems. The line of demarcation between them is not always clear.[64] None of them, however, is concerned with a choice of law; in all of them a choice of law has taken place, if a question of private law is in issue, or the operation of foreign public law has been acknowledged as a fact, if the issue is one involving public law.[65] Yet owing to the circumstance that different aspects of a situation may be governed by different legal systems (dépeçage) [65a] a reconciliation between various institutions of the several legal systems applicable in the circumstances may be called for. Thus a will which is to be interpreted according to German law may contain the appointment of a *Vorerbe* and a *Nacherbe* in respect of land in England where this institution is unknown. Here a *transposition* is called for. It will be necessary to interpret the will in the light of German law and to create interests in England which are as nearly as possible identical with those created by the will framed in accordance with another legal system and expressed in terms of different institutions.[66]

61. *Substitution* may be illustrated by reference to an intestate succession which is governed by a legal system equating adopted children with legitimate children by allowing them equal shares. If the deceased had adopted a child in accordance with another system of laws, then even if the adoption is recognised by the law governing the succession, it remains necessary to examine whether the foreign adoption represents an equivalent substitute for the type of adoption envisaged by the law governing the succession by conferring upon the adopted person a status of a legitimate child in all respects. Such equivalence is not necessarily assured by the circumstance that both legal systems acknowledge adoption as an institution, for this can vary very much in character from country to country. *Adoptio plena, minus quam plena, légitimation adoptive* and other types, are all aspects of the genus adop-

tion, but they may differ so much in effect as to exclude any interchange.[67] If the law governing the status of spouses permits the conversion of legal separations and divorces, the question may arise whether a previous legal separation abroad qualifies for this purpose.[68]

62. It is thus clear that problems of transposition and substitution arise not simply after a choice of law has taken place in accordance with the Private International Law of the *forum* which has led to the application of different systems of law to different aspects of the case. In the case of *transposition* the disparate institutions representing different aspects of the case must be translated in terms of each other. In the case of *substitution*, the question is whether the institutions representing the same aspect of the case correspond to each other to such an extent as to be interchangeable. In both cases the problem is one of comparing institutions of domestic law in order to integrate the different aspects of the case after the rules of Private International Law of the forum have led to the application of different legal systems to these various aspects or, alternatively, if the rules of public law of various legal systems have operated in their various legal spheres.[69]

63. *Adaptation* raises questions of another kind.[70] If different aspects of a case are governed by different legal systems, the operation of different laws may create hardships and material injustice. The following example illustrates the problem well. Spouses are domiciled in a common law country such as England during their working life. Upon their retirement they acquire a domicile in California. The husband dies. According to the law of California matrimonial property relations between spouses are governed by the law of the domicile of the spouses at the time of the marriage; succession to movables is governed by the law of the last domicile. According to the law of the common law State, the matrimonial régime was separation of goods, but the surviving spouse is accorded a share in her spouse's estate on the latter's death. According to the law of California spouses live according to a régime of community of goods, but a spouse is not entitled to a share in the other's estate by virtue of the law of succcession. The result is that both the law of the common law State and the law of California grant a spouse some share in the assets of the other, but by applying the common law rule to matrimonial property relations (because it was the law of their domicile at the time) and the law of California to the succession (because it was the law of the last domicile of the deceased), the sur-

viving spouse goes away with empty hands. In the converse case she collects twice over.[71] The result is not due to a faulty technique of the conflict of laws, but to the fact that each legal system is a coherent whole. Choice of law, which leads to the application of different laws to different aspects of the case, may cause a disequilibrium of solutions, but it is for the domestic law of succession to redress the balance by a process of adaptation.[72]

Section 30. Renvoi

64. It is unnecessary to set out once more the various approaches to the application of foreign law; whether the reference is to the domestic law of the *lex causae* (one step), to the domestic and private international law of the *lex causae* (simple *renvoi*, two step) or to the law which would be applied by the *lex causae* in similar circumstances (total *renvoi*, the valse, commonly known as the foreign court theory of English courts). All of these have been analysed here over the years.[73] Instead it is proposed to examine the place of *renvoi* in a system of Private International Law.

Although all countries have rules of Private International Law, these differ from each other, especially in the choice of connecting factors. This is natural since, as was shown above, Private International Law is part of the law of each country and is unfettered by any overriding uniform principles. Thus if the Private International Law of the forum refers in a particular case to some foreign legal system, it could be assumed that this reference is final. International Law does not, and foreign law cannot, impose upon the forum the duty to apply any law other than that which these courts are bound to apply in virtue of their own laws. Yet this seemingly convincing answer is only acceptable, if the premise is correct, namely, that a reference to foreign law by the Private International Law of the forum must clearly be understood to exclude the Private International Law of the *lex causae*.

In practice, *renvoi* appears to arise when one party relies on the *lex causae*, and the other on the latter's rules of Private International Law; this practical experience is not restricted to common law countries where the parties must plead foreign law, but seems to be equally valid in countries where the court can make a choice of law *proprio motu*. Here the court takes the place of one of the parties. Faced with a choice between the foreign *lex causae* and another law (*lex fori* or the law of a third country) the question is whether the reference back or on is to be accepted. At this stage it is useful to recall the problem stated above: [74] is the law of the forum a closed and self-sufficient system, with the result that it applies even to situations containing a foreign element which come before the courts, unless a specific rule of the Private International Law of the forum restricts the operation of the *lex fori* and at the same time introduces foreign law as an exception? Alternatively, is the law of the forum primarily restricted to situations having a connection with the forum on personal or territorial grounds with the result that a broad range of rules of Private International Law must determine which foreign law is applicable? Otherwise no legal system might be applicable or only the *lex fori*. No clear answer can be given, but today the second approach appears to be more favoured.

65. On this latter assumption it would seem that in the last resort the particular dispute involving a foreign element must be solved by the forum as it would be decided in the country of the *lex causae*, and not (as might be done if the first assumption were correct) by the *lex causae* if no foreign element were involved. To hold otherwise would mean to apply foreign law as applied to a hypothetical case and not as it would be applied in the individual fact situation before the court. Given this need, *renvoi* is not a problem of legal theory [75] but of practical necessity. Properly analysed, on the assumption that the *lex fori* is not closed and self-sufficient, the problem is therefore whether the *lex fori* rejects *renvoi* rather than whether it accepts it.

It must be admitted that, given the diversity of connecting factors employed by the world's systems of Private International Law, universal harmony of decision cannot be achieved. It must be stressed, however, that at least unilaterally, in one country, a fair degree of uniformity of decision with that in the country of the *lex causae* (selected by connecting factors peculiar to the *lex fori* and without universal validity) is reached by this method.

In practice the solutions in the various countries range from the complete rejection of *renvoi*, acceptance of simple *renvoi* to total or double *renvoi* in a limited number of cases, but never in all situations. Thus there exists a fair measure of agreement that *renvoi* is excluded in the law of contract [76] and tort. At the present time unsolved problems in this field include that whether *renvoi* should be admitted in the Private International Law of contract, if the parties have not exercised an express or implied choice.[77] Another new problem is that concerning the so-called "concealed" *renvoi*.[78] This is said to arise when the Private International

Law of the forum refers to foreign law, and the foreign law (mainly common law) regards the question as one of jurisdiction, treats jurisdiction and choice of law as co-extensive and attributes jurisdiction to the *forum*. In these circumstances it is said that the attribution of jurisdiction to the courts of the *forum* equals a reference back to the *lex fori*.

In the case when a civil law country, e.g., Germany, is the *forum*, instances include proceedings in Germany between American or English spouses domiciled there concerning the custody of a child of the marriage. A reference to the personal law of the spouses (to the law of a state of the U.S.A. or England) is said to be met by a jurisdictional attribution of competence to the courts in Germany, and thus to imply a reference to German law. Similar situations, it is argued, may arise in connection with divorces and ancillary claims arising therefrom, as well as in cases of adoption governed by English or American law. It is questionable whether in such circumstances a reference to the English or American law of divorce or adoption can be more than a reference to the English or American domestic law of divorce or adoption, and not the law of jurisdiction. It is true that English or American courts, if seized, would have had to decline jurisdiction, and thus also to decline the application of English or American law. But the refusal to assume jurisdiction is not equal to a reference back or on to another jurisdiction, and, *ex hypothesi*, the English or American court has never been seized at all. In other words, the reference by German law to the English or American law of divorce or adoption is a reference to the substantive law of those countries, and the refusal of English or American courts to assume jurisdiction is not a reference back or on in the field of jurisdiction, and still less in the field of substantive law. It is equally true that English or American courts will recognise a German decree of divorce or an adoption order.[79] Thus in the first case the jurisdictional problem has not arisen and cannot arise; if it did, it must be remembered that the common law rule of jurisdiction is strictly unilateral [80] and does not purport to shift jurisdiction and thus, by implication, the law applicable. In the second case a choice of law problem does not arise. Thus *renvoi*, even of the concealed kind, does not come into play. It is difficult to envisage a situation in which this problem could be raised in an English court, except in the circumstances of section 1 of the Adoption Act 1958 or of *Armitage* v. *Att.-Gen.*[81] The former would equal a choice of the foreign law of the domicile. If according to the latter (say Ontario law), the courts of the parties' residence (e.g., England) have jurisdiction, the reference back to English law is said to be implied. In reality, the

English court cannot assume jurisdiction on a reference by foreign law, and the implied reference back to English law does not operate. If English courts recognise a divorce granted by the courts in South Dakota, because it is recognised by courts of the domicile, New York, a question of recognising a foreign decree, but not a reference or transmission by foreign (New York) law is involved.

Section 31. Preliminary Question

66. It has been known for a long time that different aspects of a case involving foreign elements may be governed by different systems of laws (*dépeçage*). Thus the form of a marriage is governed by the *lex loci celebrationis* and capacity by the law of the respective domiciles of the parties. Sometimes these various aspects may have to be considered in the same case, and at times they may be connected by a relationship in which one of the aspects is of primary importance because it embodies the substance of the claim, while another affects the solution because it answers a preliminary or incidental question. Thus a claim to share in the estate of a deceased may depend upon the legitimacy of the claimant, upon the validity of a marriage to the deceased or of an adoption. The validity of a marriage may depend upon the validity of a previous divorce, and the legitimacy of a child may in turn depend upon both.

Until the end of the 1930s all these questions were regarded as posing essentially the same problem, namely as to what law applies to each individual aspect of the case according to the rules of Private International Law of the *forum*. Following the researches of Melchior,[82] Wengler [83] and Raape,[84] Robertson [85] introduced the problem into the Anglo-American world whether the choice of law for the solution of a preliminary or incidental question was to be determined not by the Private International Law of the *lex fori*, but of the *lex causae* of the principal question.

The examination of this problem is rendered more difficult by the fact that in the preponderant number of instances, the *lex fori* coincided with the *lex causae*.[86] A choice between the two alternatives raises not only a technical question, however, but one of practical importance. If the Private International Law of the *lex fori* applies, the individual substantive question which forms the object of the preliminary or incidental question in the case before the court will be determined uniformly in the *forum*, irrespective of whether or not the substantive problem arises as a principal or as a preliminary question. If the Private International Law of the *lex causae* governing the principal question applies, the individual substantive question which forms the object of the preliminary or incidental question in the case before the court will be determined differently according as the substantive problem is raised as a principal or as an incidental question. In the former case the Private International Law of the *forum*, in the latter the Private International Law of the *lex causae* applies. It would seem that the second alternative is to be preferred. Excessive importance should not be attached to the result that the same substantive question is determined by a different legal system as the circumstances lay in which it is raised before the court, even if the same person may thus be legitimate for one purpose and not for another. Such was the result of the decisions of the Canadian courts in *Schwebel* v. *Ungar*,[87] although the reasons given here are not adduced expressly.

67. It may be asked why this problem is raised when a preliminary or incidental question comes up for decision and not in other situations calling for the application of foreign law. In order to provide an answer, three possible situations must be distinguished:

(1) One single legal question only is in issue—e.g., as to what law governs succession. Here the view was taken above that in principle the *lex causae* including its rules of Private International Law should be taken into account unless the *lex fori* excludes *renvoi* expressly; the reasons are set out above.[88]
(2) Several legal questions are in issue—e.g., because claimants to the estate of a deceased person rely in part on the law governing matrimonial property relations and in part on the law governing the succession. These legal questions are of equal importance and independent of each other. Although it would be desirable to dovetail the results which follow from the application of one legal system to determine the question based on the matrimonial property régime and another based on the law of succession, no technical manipulation of the rules of Private International Law can achieve this harmony; sometimes the process of adaptation may help.[89]
(3) Several legal questions are in issue, of which all but one form preliminary or incidental questions.

It has been shown above that in these circumstances problems of substitution may occur (such as when a right of succession depends upon the validity of a foreign adoption). But in such a case the selection of the law applicable has taken place already. The question for discussion here arises at an earlier stage, if at all. To take a classic example: the court in England is called upon to determine the following case: the *de cuius*, a Greek national, who died domiciled in Greece leaving movables in England, had married the claimant in a civil marriage ceremony in England. According to Greek law, a Greek national who is a member of the Greek Orthodox Church cannot marry otherwise than in a Greek Church, and the marriage is void. Consequently, the claim of the wife to share in the estate fails. If English Private International Law is applied to both questions, the succession is governed by Greek law as the *lex ultimi domicilii*, and the validity of the marriage is (possibly) governed by English law as the *lex loci celebrationis*.[90] It is conceivable, however, that the requirement of a religious marriage ceremony laid down by Greek law is to be characterised as a matter of capacity—and Greek law is applied to this question as well. The same result will be reached if the *lex causae* governing the succession (i.e., the Greek law) including its rules of Private International Law is applied. In these circumstances a functional characterisation renders the need unnecessary to rely on the conflict rules of the law governing the main question. A further advantage of this technique is that it ensures a uniform course of decision in the *forum*, irrespective of whether the question is posed as a main question or as a preliminary question.

The difference in treatment by the conflict rules of the *forum* and of the *lex causae* may however be due to factors other than a difference of characterisation of the preliminary question. Differences in the use and characterisation of connecting factors, in the approach to *renvoi* and possibly in a number of other cases exercise an effect.[91] Here the question arises whether the *forum* should adhere to its own conflict rule to determine the preliminary question. This must depend not so much on the *lex causae* than on the evaluation of the importance of the conflict rule of the *forum*. If the latter does not express a principle which is of paramount importance to the *lex fori* as a whole, the *lex causae* including its conflicts rules should prevail over those of the *lex fori*.[92] The principle which has been developed above in connection with *renvoi* can be called in aid a second time.[93] If, however, the conflicts rule of the *forum* is determined by considerations of paramount importance to the *forum*, the fact that the *lex causae* and its conflicts rule would reach a different result is irrelevant.[94] The following example may serve as an illustration.

For a long time legitimacy in English law depended exclusively upon the existence of a valid marriage of the parents and was regarded as identical with birth in lawful wedlock according to English domestic, or, later, also according to English Private International Law. Consequently, in *Shaw* v. *Gould*,[95] which turned on the legitimacy of issue to take under a will, succession presented the main question: the validity of the marriage of the parents was treated as a preliminary question, since it alone determined legitimacy according to English law. For this purpose the English rules of the conflict of laws were applied to determine its validity, and the further preliminary question whether a previous divorce in Scotland was to be recognised was also determined according to English Private International Law.[96]

The same principle would have been applied if either legitimacy or the recognition of a foreign divorce had arisen as a principal question. In either situation the criteria constituting the operative facts of the two rules were regarded as being of paramount interest to English law. Today, a change of attitude has taken place in English law. Legitimacy is no longer determined exclusively by the existence of a valid marriage and children of voidable,[97] void [98] and subsequent [99] marriages may enjoy this status. The time may have come, therefore, to regard the intimate link between marriage and legitimacy as severed in English law and to treat them as distinct questions governed by two separate conflicts rules of the forum, which concern legitimacy on the one hand [100] and the validity of the marriage on the other hand.[101] Also, the time may be ripe to concede to the foreign *lex causae* governing legitimacy the faculty to apply its own criteria for determining legitimacy by applying the conflicts rules of the foreign law governing legitimacy to determine any preliminary questions. It is true that the law governing legitimacy may itself rely upon the validity of the marriage of the parents, but in this case the validity of the marriage has become a preliminary question to be determined by the conflicts rules governing the main question, namely, legitimacy.[102] On this view it is no longer possible to state with certainty that a marriage which is valid according to English Private International Law will result in the legitimacy of the children.[103]

The principles developed here may be tested against the instructive example given by Wolff.[104]

> "An Italian couple (A and B) validly married under all laws concerned is domiciled in England. B obtained from the English court a decree of divorce under English law on the ground of her husband's adultery. Then both parties marry again in England.

Later A goes with this second wife C to Italy, acquires a domicile there and dies leaving movable property in England."

Italian law did not at the time admit or recognise divorces of Italian citizens.[105] In proceedings in England, the determination of the preliminary question whether B or C is the wife of the *de cuius* entitled to a share in his estate, if made in accordance with the rules of Private International Law of the main question, must result in the recognition of B as the sole wife of A. It would seem, however, that where a marriage entered into in England after a divorce there is concerned, English courts will determine the validity of such a marriage according to the English rules of Private International Law. The grant of a decree of divorce in England, followed by a marriage ceremony there, especially if the other spouse is domiciled in England, appears to justify the paramountcy of English law including English Private International Law. In England [106] and in Germany,[107] the courts, when faced with a divorce of Italians in Switzerland and a subsequent attempt to enter into a second marriage in England or Germany respectively, have dealt with these two problems as separate principal questions. The result was that the Swiss divorce was recognised, but the party whose divorce was thus accepted was not allowed to marry again, because Italian law at the time forebade divorces and remarriages of their nationals. Since neither English nor German law had a paramount interest in making the effect of the Swiss divorce prevail over the incapacity to marry again according to Italian law, the result is explicable but not desirable. Consequently the Hague Convention of 1968 on the Recognition of Divorces and Legal Separations of 1 June 1970 has created a régime of the type advanced here.[108]

68. Incidental or preliminary questions in the conflict of laws have hitherto been regarded as restricted to questions of private law. However, this is not necessarily so, for they may also involve matters outside private law which are commonly said to be of a public law nature. In this case the preliminary question may be said to constitute a datum, seeing that foreign public law cannot be applied.[109] Thus a foreign rule of the road or of the high seas [110] may have to be taken into account in order to determine whether or not a person whose liability is governed by another legal system has offended against a standard of care. Similarly, in order to ascertain whether a foreign pilot was a compulsory pilot it may be necessary to examine whether according to for-

eign law a duty existed to accept the pilot and to submit to his orders,[111] and a foreign prohibition forbidding the performance of certain transactions may excuse the failure to perform a contract governed by English law.[112] The question has been put whether the last-mentioned conclusion reflects the respect for a foreign datum [113] or a rule of Private International Law of the *forum*.[114] While the practical consequence is the same, no matter which explanation is preferred, if the contract is governed by the *lex fori*, it is of importance when it is governed by a foreign legal system other than that of the place of performance. If the prohibition in the country of performance is taken into account by the *forum*, because a rule of Private International Law of the *forum* so requires, the result must be the same if the contract is governed by a foreign *lex causae*. If, however, the prohibition is treated as a datum, it can only be taken into consideration if the law governing the contract attaches consequences to it.

The answer to the question which solution is the correct one must depend upon whether or not a prohibition by the law of the place of performance is regarded as so intimately linked to the contract and thus to the law governing the contract that it must be treated as a preliminary or incidental question. On the other hand, if such a prohibition is regarded as always relevant in the *forum*, no matter whether the contract is governed by the *lex fori* or foreign law, it is obvious that a separate rule of Private International Law of the forum is required.[115]

69. Conversely, incidental or preliminary questions of a private law character may be raised by rules of public law.[116] Since the latter are self-delimiting [117] and do not contain, or rely on, choice of law rules, the question whether any legal notions employed by them refer to institutions of domestic law only or also to the same institutions in foreign law must remain a matter of construction.[118] Yet irrespective of whether the notion employed by the rule of public law of the *forum* includes the same notions abroad or not, the latter must be taken into account in one form or another. If the reference to foreign law is clear, the foreign institution must be taken into account in virtue of the reference to it; if there is no reference to foreign institutions, any foreign situations corresponding to the domestic notion will be taken into account as *data*. In either case it may be necessary to resort to the process of *substitution* [119] in order to determine whether the institutions are interchangeable.

70. In substance a conflict of laws in time can arise in one of three forms. The rule of Private International Law of the forum, or the situation attracting the connecting factor, or the *lex causae* may change. Of these, changes in the *lex causae* present much the most important and difficult problems of time in the conflict of laws, especially when the change purports to have retrospective effect.[121] In fact, the so-called retroactive effect resolves itself into two separate effects. Either the subsequent legislation purports to affect *ex nunc* the previously existing situation,[122] or *ex tunc*. Only the latter effect can properly be regarded as retroactive. Thus two different questions must be put: the first is whether the law applies to an existing legal relationship; if the first is answered affirmatively, the second is whether the law applies *ex tunc*. The first involves a question of the conflict of laws in time; the latter involves the interpretation of domestic law found to apply to an existing legal relationship.

It is generally believed that the *lex causae* should be applied in its entirety,[123] and much thought has been expended by writers on domestic law to determine in what circumstances supervening legislation is to be applied, with or without retroactive effect, to situations which have materialised previously, in the absence of specific indications that the rule is to have retrospective effect. The results of this investigation in what may be called the two-dimensional field can be put to use where the situation becomes three-dimensional through the addition of space in the form of rules of Private International Law.[124] If it is admitted that, in the sphere of one legal system alone, subsequent legislation applies to past occurrences, if they represent a continuous relationship [125] the question whether such subsequent legislation applies in space presupposes, once again, that the relationship is continuous. If it is not, as for instance in the case of succession, where the law of the last domicile (or nationality) of the deceased operates upon his death (at least in respect of movables) and as a result of it, or in the law of tort where the *lex loci delicti* or the *lex fori* or even the law governing the relationship between the parties is determining, any subsequent legislation must be disregarded,[126] because it does not apply to an event which has spent itself and does not constitute a continuous relationship. If the relationship is continuous until performed, such as a contract, it is subject to any subsequent changes in the law applicable.[127] At the same time it must be remembered that even when a relationship is continuous, subsequent legislation may not be applicable because it may have to be characterised differently, with the result that the subsequent legislation is covered by another rule of the conflict of laws and that some other legal system applies to the latter.[128] Thus the merger of two companies and the creation of a new company may be governed by the law of the country where the companies are incorporated; a subsequent statute enacted by the country of the place of incorporation discharging the new company of all debts incurred by the predecessor companies is governed by the law applicable to the respective contractual obligations.[129]

If these principles are accepted, the personal law of the deceased at the time of his death (Paraguayan law) was applied correctly to a will disposing of movable estate in England, and subsequent Paraguayan legislation declaring the estate to be property of the Paraguayan nation was rightly disregarded,[130] for both reasons indicated above: the death crystallised the law of succession, and the subsequent legislation was characterised not as falling within the field of succession but of expropriation. The latter was governed by the *lex situs*, English law, and not by the law of the last domicile of the deceased, which was Paraguayan.[131]

With equal justification the personal law of the testatrix, Austrian law, as it was in force at the time of her death, was applied in *Re Aganoor's Trusts* [132] to a settlement in the nature of substitutions contained in the will which was valid according to Austrian law in force at the time but had been invalidated by subsequent legislation of the Italian successor State. The fund was situated in England, where it had been paid into court and where successive interests were lawful. Thus the will, valid according to the law of the testatrix's domicile at the time of her death, could be given effect in England since the *lex situs*, English law, which determined the nature of the proprietary interests in the hands of the beneficiaries, allowed interests in the nature of substitutions.[133]

On the other hand, in *Nelson* v. *Bridport* [134] Sicilian law as it stood at the time of the action (and prohibited substitutions) and not as it stood at the time of the testator's death (when substitutions were lawful) was applied to a will containing a settlement of land in Sicily. However, Sicilian law was both the law governing the succession and the *lex situs* governing the nature of proprietary interests in the hands of the beneficiaries. Thus a subsequent change of Sicilian law altering the nature of the proprietary interests created some time previously and now vested in the succeeding beneficiaries had to be taken into account, because proprietary rights are governed by the *lex situs*, irrespective of the validity of the will. The latter remained valid but had become ineffective.[135] Any charge of "petrification" is inappropriate, since the *lex situs* can impose modifications of the proprietary interests in the hands of the beneficiaries at any time.

Both cases show once again that subsequent legislation which modifies previous law may have to be characterised differently from the law which it purports to modify. The former may concern a question of succession, the latter may vary the nature of proprietary interests available to be held *inter vivos*, or it may involve expropriation; the former may deal with the creation, merger or extinction of companies, the latter with the discharge of contracts entered into by these companies.

NOTES TO PART III

1. Robertson, *Characterization in the Conflict of Laws* (1940), pp. 243-244.
2. Nussbaum, *Private International Law* (1942), pp. 70-73.
3. Unger (1952), *Modern L.R.*, 88; (1959), 43 *Transactions of the Grotius Society*, 37; (1967), 83 *L.Q.R.*, 427; Mann, *Hague Rec.* 111 (1964 I), 1, at pp. 69-70; Cavers, *The Choice of Law Process* (1965), 221. Francescakis calls some of them "règles d'application immédiate". *Théorie du renvoi* (1958), 11-16, Nos. 7-11; *Rev. crit. d.i.p.*, 1966, 1; *Riv. dir. int. priv. e proc.*, 3 (1967) 691.
4. Morris (1946), 62 *Law Q.L.* 170.
5. De Nova, *Dir. Int.* 1959, 13, 500; *Mélanges Maury*, I (1960), 377; (1966), 54 *Calif. L.R.*, 1569. See Lipstein (1949), 26 *B.Y.I.L.* 553-555 and the extensive lit. cited [1972 B], 31 *Cambridge L.J.*, p. 72, n. 37; and (1977), 26 *International and Comparative Law Quarterly*, 885 nn. 10-18; see also von Mehren, (1974), 88 *Harv. L.R.*, 347; Mann (1972-73), 46 *British Yearbook of International Law*, 117, (1975); Sedler (1976), *S. Calif. L.R.*, 27; Lando (1976), 11 *Texas Int. L.J.*, 505.
6. Including legitimacy and legitimation.
7. Including their creation, powers, existence and dissolution.
8. Including their conclusion, validity, interpretation, discharge, damages.
9. Including inter-spousal immunity, effect of death upon a ciaim in tort, contributory negligence, heads and measure of damages, to mention a few aspects.
10. Created *inter vivos* and on death.
11. See Rabel, *Conflict of Laws*, I (1945), p. 42; (2 ed. 1958), p. 47; Falconbridge, *Conflict of Laws* (2 ed. 1954), p. 44; Makarov, *Vom Deutschen zum Europäischen Recht, Festschrift für Dölle*, II (1963), 149, at p. 157, n. 7. Other terms in current use are *Rahmen-* or *System-* or *Sammel-* or *Verweisungsbegriffe*—see Neuhaus, *Grundbegriffe des Internationalen Privatrechts* (1962), p. 52; *catégories de rattachement synthétiques*: Rigaux, *Théorie des qualifications en d.i.p.* (1956), No. 157, p. 244; cp. Evrigenis, *Hague Rec.* 118 (1966 II), 309, at p. 318.
12. *Points de rattachement, Anknüpfungsmomente.*
13. See Mann, *Juristenzeitung* 1956, 466; Neuhaus, *Grundbegriffe*, p. 151.
14. See Lipstein [1965], *Cambridge Law Journal*, 224, at pp. 225-226 with exemples; Neuhaus, *loc. cit.*, p. 155; Nadelmann (1969), 47 *Texas L.R.*, 765; De Winter, *Hague Rec.* 128 (1969 III), 346 at pp. 419-436.
15. E.g., status is governed by the law of the domicile; title to movables is

governed by the law of the *situs*.

16. E.g., a foreign tort can be made the object of a suit in England, if it is actionable in England *and* abroad. See also Neuhaus, *loc. cit.*, pp. 96 ff.

17. E.g., the formalities of a contract are governed *either* by the *lex loci actus* *or* by the law which governs the substance of the contract.

18. For England see *Re Annesley* [1926], Ch. 692.

19. *Badische Anilin und Soda Fabrik* v. *Basle Chemical Works Bindschedler* [1898], A.C. 200, 207; *Hanson* v. *Dixon* (1906), 23 T.L.R. 56; *Benaim* v. *Debono* [1924], A.C. 514, 520; see also *Cowan* v. *O'Connor* (1888), 20 Q.B.D. 640; *Clarke* v. *Harper* [1938], N.I. 162, 171; but contracts by telex or telephone are treated as made *inter praesentes* at the place where the answer is received: *Entores Ltd* v. *Miles Far East Corporation* [1955], 2 Q.B. 327; *N.V. Handel Mij. J. Smits* v. *English Exporters Ltd* [1955], 2 Ll.R. 69, 71; 317, 323, 324 (C.A.); and the place where it has been concluded according to these principles determines whether it has been validly concluded: *Albeko Schuhmaschinen A.G.* v. *The Kamborian Shoe Machine Co.* (1961), 111 L.J. 519; *Clunet* 1965, p. 459.

When ascertainment of the conditions underlying a connecting factor involves a question of capacity to act, it is debatable whether the matter is one for the domestic law of the *lex fori* (e.g. the United Kingdom Domicile & Matrimonial Proceedings Act 1973, s. 3 (a)) or of its rules of the conflict of laws, see Graveson (1950), 3 *International Law Quarterly*, 149.

20. See the Hague Conventions on the Form of Wills, 1961, Art. 1 *(d)*; on Jurisdiction, Applicable Law and Recognition of Decrees relating to Adoption of 1965, Arts. 2, 3, 7; and on the Recognition of Divorces and Legal Separations, 1970, Art. 2.

See also Nadelmann (1969), 47 *Texas L.R.*, 766.

21. See Makarov, *Mélanges Maury*, I (1960), 207 ff., at pp. 217, 223, and in *Vom Deutschen zum Europäischen Recht, Festschrift für Dölle*, II (1963), 149, at p. 167. The Hague Convention on the Recognition of Divorces and Legal Separations of 1970, Art. 3, has introduced a concession to common law countries by allowing the country where the matrimonial cause is tried to substitute the notion of domicile for that of habitual residence in determining its jurisdiction under the Convention; at the same time all other countries cannot refuse recognition on this ground (Art. 6, last para.).

22. *Re Annesley* [1926], Ch. 692, but see *Re O'Keefe* [1940], Ch. 124; Falconbridge, *Conflict of Laws* (2 ed. 1954), p. 208, note m; (1941), 19 *Canadian Bar Rev.*, 320, 323; de Nova, *Il Ricchiamo di ordinamenti Plurilegislativi* (1940), pp. 108 ff.

23. For a strict differentiation between the interpretation of connecting factors and characterization of operative facts see Makarov, *loc. cit.* (above n. 21), p. 151, n. 7.

24. It is generally said that common law courts apply foreign law only if pleaded and proved by the parties while civil law courts apply foreign law of their own motion. Thus formulated the difference of the practice is too clear-cut.

25. See Zajtay, *Riv. dir. int. e proc.*, 4 (1968), 233-301, esp. pp. 246-251, para. 14.

26. See also Makarov, *loc. cit.* (above p. 94, n. 21), at p. 154; but see Wengler, *Rev. crit. d.i.p.*, 1954, 661, at pp. 670, 673, 682, rejecting for such countries the approach advocated here—see *loc. cit.*, pp. 666-667, 671, 674; and in *Festschrift für Martin Wolff* (1952), 337, at pp. 340, 356.

27. Falconbridge, *Conflict of Laws* (2 ed. 1954), pp. 53 ff.; (1952), 30 *Can. Bar Rev.*, 103, at pp. 114, 116 and note 49, 117; Ledermann (1951), 29 *Can. Bar Rev.*, 3, 24.

28. Cf. Robertson, p. 127; Falconbridge, *Conflict of Laws* (1947), p. 101; (2nd ed., 1954), p. 59, believes that the court provisionally consults foreign law before finally characterising the question for the purpose of selecting the proper law. See the valid critique in Dicey, *Conflict of Laws* (8th ed., 1967), p. 27. The present account avoids this pitfall by analysing the concrete situation.

29. E.g., contract, tort, succession, capacity to marry, formality.

30. E.g., status, rights in movables or immovables, evidence, procedure, property relations between spouses.

However, according to a widely held opinion, the character of objects as immovable is determined by the *lex situs.*

31. It is assumed that the application is opposed by the other party, who alleges that another legal system is applicable.

32. In order not to complicate or to confuse this analysis no mention is made at each stage that the same process applies, if the defendant relies for his defence on the *lex fori.* Here again the court must apply its own rules of Private International Law (which are not always expressed in terms of the domestic law of the forum) in order to determine whether the *lex fori* applies; for the English practice see Lipstein [1972 B], 31 *Cambridge Law Journal,* 67, at p. 78, n. 76.

33. Where English courts have followed this technique the result has been unfortunate. See *Ogden* v. *Ogden* [1907], P. 46 (C.A.), and the comments in Dicey and Morris, pp. 237-239; Westlake, *P.I.L.* (2nd ed., 1925), p. 61; *Phrantzes* v. *Argenti* [1960], 2 Q.B. 19.

34. See Lipstein, note to *Re Maldonado* [1954], P. 223; [1954], *Cambridge Law Journal,* 123; and compare *In re Utassi's Will,* 15 N.Y. 2d 436, 209 N.Y. 2d 65 (1965), discussed by Ehrenzweig, *Hague Rec.* 124 (1968 II), 169, at p. 234, see also Ehrenzweig in *XXth Century Comparative and Conflicts of Law* (1961), 395, at pp. 402, 403, n. 4, citing *Estate of Turton,* 20 Misc. 2d 569, 192 N.Y.S. 2d 254 (Surr. 1959).

35. Cp. Graulich, *Principes de droit international privé* (1961), No. 130, p. 99, whose solution comes near to that proposed here.

36. BGHZ, 12 January 1967, N.J.W. 1967 1171, *I.P.Rspr.* 1961-1967, No. 19, p. 64; see also BGHZ 29, 137, *I.P.Rspr.* 1958-1959, No. 116, p. 389; and see Castel (1961), 39 *Can. Bar Rev.*, 93, 102 citing *Livesley* v. *Horst* [1924], S.C.R. 605; [1925] 1 D.L.R. 159.

37. *Re Cohn* [1945], Ch. 5, where according to Master Jacob in Smit, *International Co-operation in Litigation* (Europe) (1965), p. 103, n. 205, the parties agreed not to plead foreign law and to leave the question of foreign law to the court; *Re Fuld* [1966], 2 W.L.R. 717, at pp. 735, 736-738. Ehrenzweig, *XXth Century Comparative and Conflicts Law* (1961), 395, at p. 408, n. 2, does less than justice to the former decision.

38. For examples taken from English practice see *British Linen Co.* v. *Drummond* (1830), 10 B. & C. 903; *Huber* v. *Steiner* (1835), 2 Bing. N.C. 202, 210, 213; *Don* v. *Lippman* (1837), 5 Cl. & F. 1, 13, 16; *Leroux* v. *Brown* (1852), 12 C.B. 801, 823; *Bristow* v. *Sequeville* (1850), 5 Ex. 275; *Re Martin, Loustalan* v. *Loustalan* [1900], P. 211, 230, 233, 240; *S.A. de Prayon* v. *Koppel* (1933), 77 S.J. 80; *Re Cutcliffe's Will Trust* [1940], Ch. 565; *Re Middleton's Settlement* [1947], Ch. 329, 583 (C.A.); [1949], A.C. 418; *Re Priest* [1944], Ch. 58; *Adams* v. *National Bank of Greece* [1961], A.C. 255, 287; see also *Dreyfus (C. and H.) Foundation Inc.* v. *I.R.C.* [1956], A.C. 39; *Rae (Inspector of Taxes)* v. *Lazard Investment Co. Ltd* [1963], 1 W.L.R. 555; *Baron Inchyra* v. *Jennings (Inspector of Taxes)* [1966], Ch. 37; *Re Wilks* [1935], Ch. 645; *Re Kehr* [1951], 2 T.L.R. 788; [1951], 2 All E.R. 812; *Re Barnett's Trusts* [1902], 1 Ch. 842; *Mahadervan* v. *Mahadervan* [1964], P. 233, 241-242.

39. For examples taken from English practice see *Batthyany* v. *Walford* (1887), 36 Ch.D. 269, 278; *De Nicols* v. *Curlier* [1900], A.C. 21; *Re Bonacina* [1912], 2 Ch.D. 394, 396 (C.A.); *Phrantzes* v. *Argenti* [1960], 2 Q.B. 19, 36 and the comments in (1960), 9 *I.C.L.Q.*, 508; (1960), 23 *M.L.R.*, 446.

40. For examples taken from English practice see *Ogden* v. *Ogden* [1908], P. 46, and see also *Bliersbach* v. *McEwen* (1959), S.C. 43; *Lodge* v. *Lodge* (1963), 107 S.J. 437, and see the comments by Anton (1959), 3 *Jur. Rev. (N.S.)*, 253, 277; Carter in (1960), 36 *B.Y.I.L.*, 417; *Re Maldonado* [1954], P. 223, 231, 244 *et seq.*, but see Lipstein [1954], *C.L.J.*, 22. See also Garde Castillo, *La Institucion Desconocida en el d.i.p.* (1947), pp. 46-47.

41. See above, p. 95, No. 56.

42. For this problem see Robertson, *op. cit.*, pp. 118-134, 255-279; Cheshire, *Private International Law* (3rd ed. 1947), pp. 71-85; Falconbridge, *Conflict of Laws* (1st ed. 1947), pp. 98 *et seq.*, 107, 161 *et seq.*, 184 *et seq.*; but see (2nd ed. 1954), p. 68, note *(g)*; (1939), 17 *Can. Bar Rev.*, 369; (1941), 19 *Can. Bar Rev.*, 311 at 334; Ago, *Teoria del diritto internazionale privato* (1934), 136 ff., at p. 154; *Hague Rec.* 58 (1936 IV), 313 ff.; Frankenstein, *Internationales Privatrecht*, I (1926), 276 ff.; Fedozzi, *Diritto internazionale privato* (2 ed. 1939), pp. 193-195.

43. See, e.g., *Huber* v. *Steiner* (1835), 2 Bing. N.C. 202, 210, 213, per Tindall C.J.

44. German Supreme Court, 6 July 1934, RGZ 145, 121, at pp. 128 ff.; but see RGZ 7, 21 of 4 January 1882; RGZ 24, 383, 393 of 18 May 1889 and see RGZ 21, 13 of 8 May 1880; RGZ of 21 November 1910, *Niemeyer's Z.*, 21, p. 62.

45. Before the enactment of the Law Reform (Miscellaneous Provisions) Act, 1970, s. 1.

46. But contrast Wolff, *Private International Law* (2 ed. 1957), para. 156, p. 165. For a variant of this example, solved without difficulty by the writer, see Wolff, para. 155, p. 164.

47. See above No. 57 and see, e.g., *Bernkrant* v. *Fowler* (1961), 55 Cal. 2d 588, 360 P. 2d 906; *Grant* v. *McAuliffe* (1953), 41 Cal. 2d 859, 264 P. 2d 944; *Bournias* v. *Atlantic Maritime Co. Ltd.*, 220 F. 2d 152 (2 Cir. 1955).

48. See, e.g., Ehrenzweig, *Hague Rec.* 124 (1968 II), 169, at pp. 233 ff.; *Private International Law* (1967), pp. 113-219, paras. 52-55.

49. 12 N.Y. 2d 473, 191 N.E. 2d 279 (1963).

50. *Sayers* v. *International Drilling Co. N.Y.* [1971], 1 W.L.R. 1176; [1971], 3 All E.R. 163; Collins in (1972), 21 *International and Comparative Law Quarterly*, 320; and see Wengler in *Rev. crit. d.i.p.*, 1972, pp. 637-661; French Court of Cassation, 15 December 1969, *Thomas* v. *Cie. Erste Allgemeine*, *Rev. crit. d.i.p.*, 1971, p. 512, with lit.

51. See above, p. 93, and notes 2-5 with lit.

52. For England see: Wills Act 1861, ss. 1, 2; Merchant Shippjng Act 1894, s. 265; Carriage of Goods by Sea Act 1924, s. 1; Legitimacy Act 1926, ss. 1, 8; Inheritance (Family Provisions) Act 1938, s. 1 as amended; Law Reform (Frustrated Contracts) Act 1943, s. 1 (1); Adoption Act 1958, s. 1 (1) (5); Legitimacy Act 1959, s. 2 (2); Marriage (Enabling) Act 1960, s. 1 (3); Matrimonial Causes Act 1965, ss. 14 (2) *(a) (b)*, 24 (1) (2), 25 (1), 26 (1), 39 (1) (4), 40 (1) *(a) (b)*; Contracts of Employment Act 1963, s. 9 (1) (2) and Sched. 1, para. 1 (3); Redundancy Payments Act 1965, ss. 17, 56 (4); Mann (1966), 82 *L.Q.R.*, 316; see also (1964), 80 *L.Q.R.*, 29.

53. P. 165.

53a. See e.g., Swiss Federal Tribunal 31 October 1967, BGE 93 II 379, 385 (6b); ca. Mann (1972-73), 46 *British Yearbook of International Law*, 117, 124 ff.

54. *I.C.J. Reports 1958*, p. 52; for the lit. see above, p. 64, n. 13.

55. See, e.g., Conforti, *L'execuzione delle obbligazioni nel diritto internazionale privato* (1962), *passim*; for the practice in England see, e.g., *Re Bettinson's Question* [1956], Ch. 67; *Regazzoni* v. *Sethia* [1958], A.C. 301, and *Ralli Bros.* v. *Cia Naviera Sota y Aznar* [1920], 2 K.B. 287, as interpreted by Mann (1937), 18 *B.Y.I.L.*, 97; *The Halley* (1868), L.R. 2 P.C. 193, 202, and the cases cited by Lipstein in *Ius Privatum Gentium*, I (1969), 411, at pp. 420-422.

56. See Lipstein [1972 B], 31 *Cambridge Law Journal*, 67, at pp. 73-74.

57. See also Unger (1967), 83 *L.Q.R.*, 427, 444; Kelly (1969), 18 *Int. & Comp. L.Q.*, 249, at pp. 254 ff.

57a. Cp. Mann, *loc. cit.*, 124-127.

57b. See Mann, *loc. cit.*, 129.

57c. See also Lagarde, *Riv. dir. int. priv. e proc.*, 11 (1975), 648, 674 (30).

57d. See Mann, *loc. cit.*, 129-130.

57e. Cp. Mann, *loc. cit.*, 130-131.

58. See the decisions of the German Federal Supreme Court of 12 January 1967, *NJW* 1967, 1177; *IPRspr.* 1966-1967, No. 19, p. 64, and of 19 December 1958, BGHZ 29, 137, *IPRspr.* 1958-1959, No. 112; Kropholler, *NJW* 1968, 1561 with further references; Wengler, *Rev. crit. d.i.p.*, 1954, 661, at 683, n. 2; Ago, *Hague Rec.* 58 (1936 IV), 245, at pp. 326 ff.; Frankenstein, *Internationales Privatrecht*, I (1926), p. 285.

59. S. 5; the Wills Act 1963, s. 3, enacted by the United Kingdom; the Netherlands did not ratify this Convention.

60. See Robertson, *Characterization in the Conflict of Laws* (1940), pp. 235-237; Beckett (1934), 15 *B.Y.I.L.*, 46, at 73, n. 1; Falconbridge, *Conflict of Laws* (2nd ed., 1954), pp. 90-94; Lorenzen, *Selected Articles*, pp. 129-130; (1941), 50 *Yale L.J.*, 743, at 755, 756; and the former practice of the German Supreme Court, RG., *JW* 1913, 333.

61. [1932], P. 78.

62. [1939] A.C. 277.

62a. But contrast the Carriage of Goods by Sea Act 1971, Schedule art. X.

63. These categories were first discussed by Lewald, *Hague Rec.* 69 (1939 III), 1, at 129. For lit. see Kegel, *Internationales Privatrecht* (3 ed. 1971), p. 125.

64. According to Neuhaus, *Grundbegriffe des Internationalen Privatrechts* (1962), 251, n. 604, the category described as transposition merges into the other two. There is some substance in this contention, at least as far as any overlap between transposition and substitution is concerned.

65. Where domestic and foreign public law are concerned, the recognition of the operation of foreign law takes the place of the so-called preliminary question; see below p. 220 and see Mann (1963), 79 *Law Quarterly Review*, 525; *Hague Rec.* 132 (1971 I), 109, at pp. 134-144.

65a. See Reese (1973), 73 *Col.L.R.*, 48; Lagarde, *Riv. dir. int. priv. e proc.*, 11 (1975), 649.

66. *Studd* v. *Cook* (1883), 8 App. Cas. 577 at pp. 591, 600, 604; *Re Piercy* [1895], 1 Ch. 83, 89; *Piercy* v. *E.t.f.a.s.*, decided on 15 March 1956 by the Tribunale Oristano, *Foro it.* 1956, I, 1019; *Riv. dir. internaz.*, 1959, 687; *Re Ernst Meyer*, *Gutachten zum internationalen und ausländischen Privatrecht*, 1967 and 1968 (1970), No. 67, p. 707.

67. See *Re Marshall* [1957], Ch. 507 (C.A. and, generally, Ancel, *L'adoption dans les législations modernes* (2nd ed. 1958), and the supplement in *Rev. internat. de dr. comp.*, 13 (1961), 561.

68. See, e.g., *Tursi* v. *Tursi* [1958], P. 4; and the problems raised in the cases cited by Mann, *Hague Rec.* 132 (1971 I), at pp. 135 ff.: whether a woman validly married in a polygamous union in Pakistan according to the personal law of the

parties is a wife for the purpose of receiving public assistance in England under the National Assistance Act 1948, *Imam Din* v. *National Assistance Board* [1967], 2 Q.B. 213, at p. 218; a French *société en nom collectif* a corporate body or partnership for the purpose of English tax legislation: *Dreyfuss* v. *Commissioners of Inland Revenue* (1929), 14 T.C. 560, at pp. 576, 577; life interest in the income of a New York trust fund; whether income from stocks, shares or rents, or from other possessions outside the United Kingdom for the purposes of English tax legislation: *Archer-Shee* v. *Garland* [1931], A.C. 212, with a valid criticism by Mann, *loc. cit.*, at p. 136; a distribution of shares in a subsidiary in Maryland to the shareholders of the parent company, treated as capital in Maryland; whether a distribution of income for the purposes of English tax legislation: *Rae* v. *Lazard Investment Co.* [1963], 1 W.L.R. 555, see also *Courtaulds Investment Ltd.* v. *Fleming* [1969], 1 W.L.R. 1683. For what would appear to be the correct answer in keeping with the attitude taken above in the text see *Baron Inchyra* v. *Jennings (Inspector of Taxes)* [1966], Ch. 37.

69. See below p. 111.

70. Cp. Lewald, *Hague Rec.* 69 (1939·III), 1, at pp. 139-148; Kegel, *Internationales Privatrecht* (3 ed. 1971), pp. 127 ff.; Raàpe, *Hague Rec.* 50 (1934 IV), 401, at pp. 496-517.

71. *Baudoin* v. *Trudel* [1937], 1 D.L.R. 216; [1937], O.R. 1, but see Kegel, *Internationales Privatrecht* (3 ed. 1971), p. 129.

72. See the Californian Probate Code s. 201.5 (California Statutes 1957, c. 490); see also s. 201,7,6; 140.5 (1961) and see Kegel, *op. cit.*, pp. 131-133, with lit.; Cavers, *Hague Rec.* 131 (1970 III), 75, at p. 215, n. 57, 58; Abel, Berry, Halsted and Marsh, 47 *Calif. L.R.*, 211 (1959).

Leflar, (1960), 99 *Trusts & Estates*, 882; Schreter (1962), 50 *Calif.L.R.*, 206; Gardner (1966), 54 *Calif.L.R.*, 252; Steindorff, *Sachnormen* (1958), 81 ff.; and compare *Re Thornton's Estate,* 1 Cal. 2d 1, 33 P. 2 d 1 (1934).

73. See in this collection of courses Lewald, *Hague Rec.* 29 (1929 IV), 515-616; 69 (1939 III), 1 at 47-66; de Nova, *Hague Rec.* 118 (1966 II), 437, at pp. 485-531, and the lit. cited by Kegel, *op. cit.*, p. 139; Ehrenzweig, *Private International Law* (1967), p. 141, n. 6, with further references; *Hague Rec.* 124 (1968 II), 167, at pp. 238-244.

74. Pp. 80-81.

75. Neither the need, existing in common law countries, for the parties to prove foreign law as it would be applied in the foreign country concerned and not abstract rules of law, nor the alleged preference of English judges for having foreign judges decide foreign cases—see de Nova, *Hague Rec.* 118 (1966 II), at pp. 500, 502-503, esp. 506, para. 25; Ehrenzweig, *Private International Law* (1967), p. 146, para. 70—provide a well-founded theoretical explanation. It was precisely his previous refusal to try a case involving a succession concerning personalty including an English leasehold interest of a *de cuius* who had died domiciled in France: *De Bonneval* v. *De Bonneval* (1838), 1 Curt 856, which led the same Judge to "sit as a foreign court" in *Collier* v. *Rivaz* (1841), 2 Curt. 855.

76. See, e.g., *Re United Railways of Havana* v. *Regla Warehouses Ltd.* [1960], Ch. 52 at pp. 96-97, 115 (C.A.); *Rosencrantz* v. *Union Contractors Ltd.* (1960), 23 D.L.R. (2d.) 473; Castel (1961), 39 *Can. Bar Rev.*, 93; (1961), 21 *Rev. du Barreau de Quebec*, 181, 189; Sherwood (1956), 5 *Am.J.Comp.L.*, 120-125; Raape, *Neue Juristische Wochenschrift* 1959, 1013, 1016; but see *Mason* v. *Rose*, 176 F. (2d) 486 (2 Cir. 1949); *Siegelman* v. *Cunard*, 221 F. (2d) 189 (1 Cir. 1955); *University of Chicago* v. *Dater*, 227 Mich. 658, 279 N.W. 175 (1936); *Alaska Airlines Inc.* v. *Stephenson*, 217 F. 2d 295 (9 Cir. 1954); ca.: *Lann* v. *United Steel Works Corpn.*, 166 Misc. 465, 1 N.Y.S. (2d) 951, 957; *Duskin* v. *Pensylvania*

Central Airlines Corp., 71 F. Supp. 867 (E.D. Pa. 1947), 167 F. 2d 727, 730 [6] (6 Cir. 1948), cert. denied 335 US 829 (1948); *Fahs* v. *Martin*, 224 F. 2d 387, 398 [9] (5 Cir. 1955); C. A. Frankfurt, 13 November 1956, *IPRspr.* 1956-1957, No. 24, affirmed by the German Supreme Court, 14 February 1958, *NJW* 1958, 750, *AWD* 1958, 57, *IPRspr.* 1958-1959, No. 39, p. 155, and of 9 June 1960, *NJW* 1960, 1720, *AWD* 1960, 183, *IPRspr.* 1960-1961, No. 23, p. 94; but see Swiss Federal Tribunal, 21 October 1955, BGE 81, II, 391.

77. See the survey by Graue, *Aussenwirtschaftdienst des Betriebsberaters* 1968, 121; Gamillscheg, 27 *Rabel's Z.* (1962), 591; Maier, *NJW* 1962, 323, 325; Kreuzer, *Das Internationale Privatrecht des Warenkaufs* (1964), 284; Hartwig, *Renvoi im international Privatrecht* (1967), 152, 156; Vischer, *Internationales Vertragsrecht* (1962), 111; Batiffol, *Conflits de Lois en matière de contrats* (1938), No. 53; *Traité de d.i.p.* (4th ed. 1967), No. 311, p. 358 and note 52 *bis*: Kegel in *Soergel's Kommentar* (10th ed., 1970), note 34 to article 27; Kelly (1969), 18 *I.C.L.Q.*, 249, at p. 257, n. 39; de Nova, *Hague Rec.* 118 (1966 II), 518-519; Ehrenzweig, *ibid.*, 124 (1968 II), 240; *Private International Law* (1967), 148-149, par. 73 ff.; Bayitch (1953), 7 *Miami L.Q.*, 312.

78. See Hanisch, *NJW* 1966, 2085, with lit. and cases p. 2086, n. 15; see especially Neuhaus, *Grundbegriffe des I.P.R.* (1962), 190-194; *JZ* 1954, 704; Gündisch, *Fam.R.Z.* 1961, 352; Jayme, *Dir. Int.*, 22 (1968), pp. 84, 88, notes 33, 34, with lit.; *Z.f.Rv.* 11 (1970), 253; Ehrenzweig, *Treatise on the Conflict of Laws* (1962), 404; *Private International Law* (1967), p. 147, para. 72. For a case of concealed reference on (transmission) see the decision of the Court of Mainz of 21 October 1966, StAZ 1967, 24; *IPRspr.* 1966-1967, No. 159, p. 502, reported by Jayme, *loc. cit.*, and in (1969), 21 *Florida L.R.*, 290; Soergel-Kegel, *Kommentar zum BGB*, Vol. VII (10th ed., 1970), note 14 to Art. 27. Von Mehren in *XXth Century Comparative and Conflicts Law* (1961), pp. 380, 382, uses the term in a different sense.

79. The situation is not unlike that in *Armitage* v. *Att.-Gen.* [1906], P. 235, which is not regarded as one involving *renvoi*. See Dicey and Morris, *Conflict of Laws*, pp. 61-62.

80. See above, pp. 45-46, 99 ff.

81. [1906], P. 135. See also *Abate* v. *Abate* [1961], P. 29; *Mather* v. *Mahoney* [1968], 1 W.L.R. 1773; [1968], 2 All E.R. 223.

82. *Die Grundlagen des deutschen international Privatrechts* (1932), pp. 249 *et seq.*

83. *Rabels Z.*, 8 (1934), 148; *Dir. Int.*, 17 (1963), I, 50; *Rev. crit. d.i.p.*, 1966, 165. See also van Hoogstraten in *Mélanges Kollewijn* (1962), p. 209; Lagarde, *Rev. crit. d.i.p.*, 1960, 459, with further lit. at n. 1. For a survey, see Voskuil (1965), 19 *Dir. Int.*, I, 183; de Nova, *Hague Rec.* 118 (1966 II), at pp. 557-569.

84. *Hague Rec.* 50 (1934 IV), 401, at pp. 485-495.

85. *Characterization in the Conflict of Laws* (1940), 135-156; (1939), 55 *L.Q.R.*, 565, at p. 584.

86. For England see *Birtwhistle* v. *Vardill* (1840), 7 Cl. & F. 940; *Re Wright's Trusts* (1856), 2 K. & J. 595; *Mette* v. *Mette* (1859), 1 Sw. & Tr. 416; *Brook* v. *Brook* (1861), 9 H.L.C. 193; *Shaw* v. *Gould* (1868), L.R. 3, H.L. 55; *Re Goodman's Trusts* (1881), 17 Ch.D. 266; *Re Andros* (1883), 24 Ch.D. 637; *Re Grove* (1888), 40 Ch.D. 216; *Re Bozelli* [1902], 1 Ch. 751; *De Wilton* v. *Montefiore* [1909], 2 Ch. 481; *Skottowe* v. *Young* (1871), L.R. 11 Eq. 474; *Atkinson* v. *Anderson* (1882), 21 Ch.D. 100; *Cantiere San Rocco* v. *Clyde Shipbuilding etc. Co.* [1924], A.C. 226; *Fibrosa Spolka Akcyjna* v. *Fairbairn Lawson Combe Barbour Ltd.* [1943], A.C. 32; *Kahler* v. *Midland Bank* [1950], A.C. 24. In the case of suretyship Voskuil, p. 192, distinguishes between preliminary and incidental questions.

87. [1963], 37 D.L.R. (2d) 467; (1964), 42 D.L.R. (2d) 622, 633; [1964], O.R. 430, 441 (C.A.); [1965], S.C.R. 148, [1965], 48 D.L.R. (2d) 644. The decision could have been supported on another ground, drawn from the principle of the conflict of laws in time: see Lipstein (1967), 2 Ottawa L.R. 49, 56, relying on arguments developed in [1967], *C.L.J.*, 42. If this approach had been chosen, the problem would have involved two principal questions of equal standing, i.e., the recognition of a divorce in Italy of Hungarian domiciliaries and the capacity to marry of a person domiciled in Israel, who had been divorced, on the strength of a decree recognised in Ontario. See also Lysyk (1965), 43 *Can. Bar Rev.*, 365; Webb (1965), 14 *I.C.L.Q.*, 659.

88. See above p. 105, No. 65.

89. See the observations above No. 63, p. 103, on the problem of adaptation.

90. See Wolff, *Private International Law* (2nd ed., 1950), ss. 196, 198, pp. 206-209.

91. Gottlieb (1955), 33 *Can. Bar Rev.*, 523, 528.

92. Lipstein (1967), 2 *Ottawa L.R.*, 49, at p. 58; see also Unger (1957), 43 *Transactions of the Grotius Society*, 86, at p. 94.

93. Cf. Wolff, *Private International Law*, s. 196.

94. Wengler, *Rabels Z.*, 22 (1958), 535, at 544, is more pragmatic.

95. (1869), L.R. 3 H.L. 55.

96. According to Inglis (1957), 6 *I.C.L.Q.*, 202, at p. 214, *Shaw* v. *Gould* turned on the validity of the first marriage, and therefore on English law as that of the domicile of the children. However, in this case the presumption of legitimacy would have applied.

97. Matrimonial Causes Act 1965, s. 11.

98. Legitimacy Act 1959, s. 2.

99. Legitimacy Act 1926, s. 1, now the Legitimacy Act 1976, s. 1.

100. See in a different context, but in a similar vein, Melchior, *Grundlagen*, p. 260, and notes 3 and 4; Lagarde, *Rev. crit. d.i.p.*, 1960, 459, at p. 468, who speaks of "éloignement". And see Wolff, *Private International Law*, paras. 362, 363.

101. Dicey and Morris, Rule 60, p. 418.

102. Subject to the modifications set out above, see Lipstein in *Festschrift für Rabel* (1954), 611.

103. E.g., a marriage valid in England under the rule in *Sottomayor* v. *De Barros (No. 2)* (1879), 5 P.D. 94.

104. *Private International Law* (2nd ed., 1950), s. 200.

105. On 18 December 1970 divorce was introduced in Italy. (Law No. 898 of 1 December 1970.) According to Art. 3 of the Law, a marriage abroad after a decree of divorce granted abroad will be recognised in respect of parties subject to Italian law.

106. *R.* v. *Brentwood Superintendent Registrar of Marriages, ex p. Arias* [1968], 2 Q.B. 956.

107. L. G. Weiden, 28 February 1953, NJW 1953, *IPRspr.* 1952-1954, No. 104; Directive of the President of the OLG Hamburg, 5 August 1955, *IPRspr.* 1954-1956, No. 84, *Rev. crit. d.i.p.*, 1957, p. 50; BGH, 12 February 1964, BGHZ 41, 136, at p. 143 (3) with lit. at p. 144, referring to OLG Karlsruhe, 3 September 1962, *IPRspr.* 1962-1963, No. 70; OLG Munich 17 December 1962, *IPRspr.* 1962-1963, No. 72; LG Cologne, 10 January 1962, *IPRspr.* 1962-1963, No. 66; see also BGH, 14 July 1966, BGHZ 46, 87, at p. 93—but see the conclusions to the contrary and concurring with those put forward above in the text by the court below.

108. Lipstein (1967), 2 *Ottawa L.R.*, 49. For the new Swiss practice see BGE

97, I, 389 of 3 June 1971; Dutoit and Mercier, *Riv. dir. int. priv. e proc.*, 8 (1972), 5.

109. See Lipstein, *Ius Privatum Gentium*, I (1969), 411, at pp. 420-421.

110. *The Halley* (1868), L.R. 2 P.C. 193, at p. 203; cf. *S.S. Diana, The Cliveden* [1894], A.C. 625, 629; *The Youri* v. *The Spearman* (1885), 10 App. Cas. 276; *The Talabot* (1890), 15 P.D. 194; *The Kaiser Wilhelm der Grosse* [1907], P. 36, 43-44; *The City of Berlin* [1908], P. 110.

111. *The Augusta* (1887), 57 L.T.R. 326, 327; *The Darlington* [1903], P. 77, 78, 80; *The Prinz Hendrick* [1899], P. 177, 181; *The Guy Mannering* (1882), 7 P.D. 132, 135; *The Agnes Otto* (1887), 12 P.D. 56, 57; *The Andoni* [1918], P. 14, 18; *The Waziristan* [1953], 2 All E.R. 1213; *The Peerless* (1860), Lush. 30; *The Arum* [1921], P. 12, 18, 20.

112. *Ralli Bros.* v. *Compania Naviera Sota y Aznar* [1920], 2 K.B. 287.

113. Mann (1937), 18 *B.Y.I.L.*, 97, 107-113; Falconbridge, *Conflict of Laws*, 387, pp. 391-394; Morris (1953), 6 *Vanderbilt L.R.*, 505 at 510; *Rabel*, II, 536; Cheshire and North, 228-229. See also Serick, *Rabels Z.*, 18 (1953) 633, 647, with reference to the decisions of the German Supreme Court RGZ 161, 296, 300; 93, 182, 184 and the lit. cit. in n. 79.

114. Dicey and Morris, Rule 132, Exception, pp. 761-762.

115. The present attitude of English law is not clear; see *Regazzoni* v. *Sethia* [1958], A.C. 301; Morris (1953), 6 *Vanderbilt L.R.*, 505, at p. 510, with references to earlier cases.

116. Mann (1963), 79 *L.Q.R.*, 525; *Hague Rec.* 132 (1971 I), 109, at pp. 134-144.

117. See above pp. 45-46, 66.

118. Mann, *loc. cit.*, above note 116.

119. See above p. 102, No. 61; Mann, *Hague Rec.* 132 (1971 I), at p. 144 (4).

120. For the lit. see Rigaux, *Hague Rec.* 117 (1966 I), pp. 433-437, especially Affolter, Batiffol, Castel, Diena, Gavalda, Grodecki, Lysyk, Makarov, Mann, Morris, Olivi, Roubier, Szászy, Spiro, *loc. cit.*

121. Dicey and Morris, *Conflict of Laws* (8 ed. 1967), p. 44.

122. Such as the English Legitimacy Act 1926, s. 8 (1), introducing *legitimatio per subsequens matrimonium.*

123. Critically Wengler, *Rabels Z.*, 23 (1958), 535, at pp. 552, 558 ff.

124. See my review of Roubier, *Le droit transitoire* (2 ed. 1960), in [1961], *Cambridge Law Journal*, 123.

125. E.g., contracts, matrimonial relations, both of a personal and of a proprietary nature and other family relationships. For the use of this distinction see Wengler, *Rabels Z.*, 22 (1958), 535, at p. 543; for its practical, application see *Parkasho* v. *Singh* [1968], P. 233.

126. Unless a positive rule of Private International Law requires the contrary, as does the rule in *Phillips* v. *Eyre* (1870), L.R. 6 Q.B. 1 at p. 28, see Lipstein [1972 B], 31 *Cambridge Law Journal*, 67, at p. 99.

127. See, e.g., *Rex* v. *International Trustee for Bondholders A.G.* [1937], A.C. 500. Dicey and Morris, *Conflict of Laws* (8 ed. 1967), p. 47, n. 44, with cases; Grodecki, *loc. cit.*, p. 78. Of course the position is different if foreign law is only incorporated into the contract which is, itself, governed by some other legal system.

128. Wengler, *Rabels Z.*, 23 (1958), 535.

129. *Adams* v. *National Bank of Greece S.A.* [1961], A.C. 255, and see Lipstein [1960], *Cambridge Law Journal*, 169.

130. *Lynch* v. *Government of Paraguay* (1871), L.R. 2 P. & D. 268, esp. p. 272.

131. *Bank voor Handel, etc.* v. *Slatford* [1953], 1 Q.B. 248, at pp. 257 *et seq.*; Diplock L.J. in *Adams* v. *National Bank of Greece and Athens* [1958], 2 Q.B. 59,

76, 77, but see Lord Reid in *Adams* v. *National Bank of Greece S.A.* [1961], A.C. 255, 282.

132. (1895), 66 L.J.Ch. 521.

133. But see Dicey and Morris, *Conflict of Laws* (8 ed. 1967), p. 45; Mann, *loc. cit.*, who argues that Italian law altered the beneficial interests in the trust fund. According to the view taken here it altered the nature of proprietary interests in general capable of being held according to Italian law as the *lex situs*. See also Grodecki, 69.

134. (1846), 8 Beav. 547.

135. The common contention that *Re Aganoor's Trusts* and *Nelson* v. *Bridport* are conflicting decisions cannot be supported.

PART IV. CONCLUSIONS

71. The purpose of these lectures was to examine the nature, the function and the structure of Private International Law. The need to determine the application of law in space has existed throughout the ages, but the aims and the methods which determine its sphere of operation have never crystallised. The nature of rules of private law, the discretion of individual legal systems, subject only to the overriding control of customary International Law, the international character of rules of Private International Law, constitutional principles which can balance the choice of law in a Federal State, sociological and teleological considerations have been called in to provide criteria of general or international validity.

The foregoing examination has shown that every one of these theories or basic ideas has re-appeared over the ages in a slightly modernised guise. Yet some fundamental insights have emerged. Unlike in the realm of public law, where governmental action is paramount and where the sphere of operation is necessarily circumscribed by the need not to impinge on the legitimate sphere of operation of other governments, private law is not so restricted. Its sphere of application, embodied in a set of rules of Private International Law, is only controlled in substance and not territorially by the general rules of Public International Law which prohibit illegal discrimination and demand the observance of minimum standards of behaviour. At the same time, Public International Law has developed a set of rules of the conflict of laws for the use of international tribunals, but these rules differ in nature and function from those which form part of domestic law, and there is no hierarchy of norms. Modern doctrines which rely on a balance of governmental interests or of substantive rules find their justification in the law and Constitution of the United States, where the law is homogeneous, the laws of the member States are on an equal footing, and the Supreme Court watches over the balancing act. Their usefulness outside such a special framework remains doubtful. In the end the exercise of discretion by individual legal systems in devising rules of Private International Law is only matched by the need to provide certainty from the outset, except perhaps where torts are involved.

In these circumstances each domestic legal system on its own, without any specific directives by Public International Law, must determine whether it will regard itself as closed, self-sufficient and complete, except where it makes specific concessions to foreign law or whether it regards itself as primarily restricted to situations having a connection of a personal or territorial character with the country of the *forum*. The trend in the United States appears to be in the former direction; that elsewhere in the world points in the latter direction.

The structure of the rules of Private International Law reflects these trends. Their formulation in terms of orthodox rules of the conflict of laws, or as spatially conditioned internal rules, their detailed or rudimentary character provides a pointer. The view appears to receive growing support that foreign law occupies a place concurrently with domestic law and that the structure of domestic rules of Private International Law may not be able to take sufficiently into account the different character of foreign law and legal institutions as well as different choice of law rules. This realisation has led to a greater emphasis on the importance of characterisation (qualification) and of *renvoi* and to the development of sophisticated solutions, and has also accorded its proper place to the preliminary question by conceding a role to the rules of Private International Law of the foreign *lex causae*. At the same time, the foreign legal system chosen as the *lex causae* is not allowed unlimited power, and subsequent foreign legislation may find its match in local rules of conflict of laws in time.

BIBLIOGRAPHY

Ago, *Teoria del d.i.p.* (1934). "Règles générales de D.I.P.", *Hague Rec.* (1936 IV), 243.

Arminjon, "La notion des droits acquis en D.I.P.", *Hague Rec.* 44 (1933 II), 1.

Batiffol, *Aspects philosophiques du droit international privé* (1956).

Batiffol (and Lagarde), *Droit international privé*, I (5 ed. 1970).

Cavers, "A Critique of the Choice-of-Law Process" (1933), 47 *Harv.L.R.*, 173.

— "Two Local Law Theories" (1950), 63 *Harv.L.R.*, 822.

— *The Choice of Law Process* (1965).

W. W. Cook, *The Logical and Legal Basis of the Conflict of Laws* (1942), esp. p. 1 ff.

Currie, B., *Selected Essays on the Conflict of Laws* (1963).

David, *La loi étrangère devant le juge du fond* (1965).

De Nova, "Historical and Comparative Introduction to Conflict of Laws", *Hague Rec.* 118 (1966, II), 434.

Dicey and Morris, *Conflict of Laws* (8 ed. 1967).

Ehrenzweig, *Treatise on the Conflict of Laws* (1962).

— *Private International Law* (1967).

— "Specific Principles of Private International Law", *Hague Rec.* 124 (1968 II), 169.

Evrigenis, "Les tendances doctrinales actuelles en D.I.P.", *Hague Rec.* 118 (1966 II), 309.

Falconbridge, *Conflict of Laws* (2 ed. 1954).

Gutzwiller, "Le developpement historique du D.I.P.", *Hague Rec.* 29 (1929 IV), 291.

Hambro, "Conflict Law as Part of International Law", in *Varia Juris Gentium, Liber amicorum J. P. François* (1959), 132.

— "The Relations between International Law and Conflict Law", *Hague Rec.* 105 (1962 I), 1.

Kahn-Freund, *The Growth of Internationalism in English Private International Law* (1962).

Kegel, *Internationales Privatrecht* (3 ed. 1971).

Lewald, "Règles générales des conflits de lois", *Hague Rec.* 69 (1939 III), 127.

— "Conflits de lois dans le monde grec et romain", *Rev. crit. d.i.p.*, 1968, 419-440, 615-639.

Lipstein, "Conflict of Laws before International Tribunals, I, II", (1942), 27 *Transactions of the Grotius Society*, 142. (1944) 29 *Transactions of the Grotius Society*, 51.

— "Recognition of Governments and the Application of Foreign Law" (1950), 35 *Transactions of the Grotius Society*, 157.

— "Conflict of Laws 1921-1971; The Way Ahead [1972 B]", 31 *Cambridge L.J.*, 67.

Lorenzen, *Selected Articles on the Conflict of Laws* (1947), esp. pp. 1 ff., 181 ff.

Mann, "The Doctrine of Jurisdiction in International Law", *Hague Rec.* 111 (1964 I), 1.

— "The Primary Question of Construction and the Conflict of Laws" (1963), 79 *Law Quarterly Review*, 525.

— "Conflict of Laws and Public Law", *Hague Rec.* 132 (1971 I), 109.

Maury, "Règles générales des conflits de lois", *Hague Rec.* 57 (1936 III), 325.

Meijers, "L'histoire des principes fondamentaux du D.I.P. à partir du Moyen Age...", *Hague Rec.* 49 (1934 III), 543.
Morris, *Conflict of Laws* (1971).
Monaco, *L'efficacia della legge nello spazio* (2 ed. 1964).
Nadelmann, "Some Historical Notes on the Doctrinal Sources of American Conflict Law", *Jus et Lex, Festgabe für Gutzwiller*, 263.
Neuhaus, *Grundbegriffe des Internationalen Privatrechts* (1962).
Neumeyer, *Die gemeinrechtliche Entwickelung des internationalen Privat- und Strafrechts bis Bartolus*, I (1901), II (1916).
Niederer, *Einführung in die allgemeinen Lehren des I.P.R.* (3 ed. 1963), cited 2 ed. 1956.
Rheinstein, "Das Kollisionsrecht im System des Verfassungsrechts der Vereinigten Staaten von Amerika", *Festschrift für Rabel*, I (1954), 539.
Robertson, *Characterization in the Conflict of Laws* (1940).
Sack, *Law, A Century of Progress*, III (1937), 322.
Shapira, *The Interest Approach to Choice of Law* (1970).
Sperduti, *Saggi di teoria generale del d.i.p.* (1967).
Stevenson, "Effect of Recognition on the Application of Private International Law Norms" (1951), 51 *Col.L.R.*, 710.
— "The Relationship of Private International Law with Public International Law" (1952), 52 *Col.L.R.*, 561.
Zajtay, *Contribution à l'étude de la condition de la loi étrangère en d.i.p. français* (1958).

TABLE OF CASES

INTERNATIONAL COURTS AND TRIBUNALS

Arbitral Tribunals

MUNICIPAL COURTS

INDEX